Arthur Burdett Frost, Octave Thanet, Margaret Armstrong, Alice French

The Heart of Toil

Arthur Burdett Frost, Octave Thanet, Margaret Armstrong, Alice French
The Heart of Toil
ISBN/EAN: 9783744666114

Printed in Europe, USA, Canada, Australia, Japan

Cover: Foto ©Thomas Meinert / pixelio.de

More available books at **www.hansebooks.com**

❦❦❦ The Heart of Toil
By Octave Thanet ❦❦❦

Illustrated by A. B. Frost

Charles Scribner's Sons
New York ~~~~~ 1898

*Copyright, 1898, by
Charles Scribner's Sons*

CONTENTS

	Page
The Non-Combatant,	1
The Way of an Election,	45
The Moment of Clear Vision,	83
Johnny's Job,	123
The "Scab,"	159
The Conscience of a Business Man,	191

LIST OF ILLUSTRATIONS

A voice cried, heartily, "Come in, Vi; what are you waiting for?" . . Frontispiece

                                    Facing page

"Johnny O'Brien's baby died this morning," 14

He had heard in Swedish, German, and Irish dialects all about the obnoxious new "Bosses," 20

The sewing-machine of Spriggs's trundled down the steps, ... 28

Relieved their chafed vanity by a few threats, ... 34

"Race, you old fool, come down!" . . 40

Leroy sat perfectly still for a few minutes, 52

LIST OF ILLUSTRATIONS

	Facing page
The Meeting,	58
"I've supplied him with literature,"	68
"He tumbled to it like a gentle bird,"	72
"I'm one of your converts,"	78
"I've got something to propose to you, boys," said Leroy,	90
"They caught them. Hughey only's got a year,"	112
"But, there, I stood scowling at him and wondering whether I wouldn't break his head,"	116
He pushed the vision out of his mind, yet he never again could be so lightly sure of his own judgment,	120
Johnny mended it,	132
"Miss Glenn's gone,"	140
"I was bathing him with it," Johnny explained, promptly,	146

LIST OF ILLUSTRATIONS   ix

Facing page

They pulled him into the boat, ... 154

"It's a shame," agreed the old woman, warmly, ... 164

"Track clear! Don't stop!" 184

And told him how the great house had been his grandfather's, ... 194

"He showed me Jabez's certificate," . . 204

What his frowning gray eyes saw was not the oaken woodwork of the office, . . 206

THE NON-COMBATANT

THE NON-COMBATANT

"WELL, won't your pa be pleased!" cried Mrs. Battles.

The slim girl with the rose-leaf complexion, and the silky black braid dangling in the hollow between her shoulders, turned quickly. The pretty flush crept from her cheeks to her forehead, her liquid dark eyes brightened and glowed.

"Will it cheer him up, do you really think, ma?" said she.

Mrs. Battles was dishing the dinner, for it was noon and time for Race Battles to come upstairs from the grocery. She waved the coffee perilously at her daughter's face, in a gesture of reproach. "Stella Battles! Don't you know no more of your pa than not to know he'll be tickled to death? There ain't a father in town wouldn't be! I should *say!*"

Stella placed the bread and the tiny mite of butter—meals did not have their former generous look at the grocer's now. She looked at the table-cloth and spoke in a soft rush, like one who fears the failing of her own courage midway: "Ma, I know he would be pleased, usually; but—he seems so changed and worried all the time now; and—and there would be the expense of the graduating dress, the gloves, and ribbons and those things——"

"Don't you fret, lambie," returned the mother, tenderly, as the girl's voice quivered and sank; "if pa can't raise the money for your graduating muslin, your ma can! And you know pa sets the world and all by your learning. But he's so beset and worried, now, he don't know which way to turn. But you see how it is, Stella, it's seven weeks now since the boys struck, and the bills are going on and on; and there don't seem no more chance now than there was the first week—not so much, even—that the strike will be settled; and however will the bills get paid? It makes the creeps come up my back when I think of it; I don't wonder there's gray hairs in Race's head nor that he groans in his sleep. I don't see how pa'd live through it to fail! He said that when he mortgaged the house, last week, and I cried when I signed. But he's got the money to pay Wells. He's the worst, that man!"

She inclined her comely head toward the open door, through which one could see all the variegated pomp of the Battles's parlor, the tapestry sofa, the columned and chamfered mantel, and the geraniums and fuchsias, behind the lace curtains. On the mantel-piece (tastefully draped in light-blue silk) were two Parian marble statuettes. One, the Battles had discovered since Stella studied Latin, represented Clytie emerging from her sunflower; the other they had always revered as the bust of Abraham Lincoln. Both works of art were bought at a bargain sale by Mr. Battles and had been preserved in a drawer and tissue-paper until the parlor was furnished. In the centre of the mantel towered grandly a bronze clock, presented by his former employers, the rich wholesale grocers, Harcourt T. Wells & Co. The other ornaments were two photographs—one, thrown on convex glass and colored, the photograph of a smiling baby boy; the other, that of a middle-aged man whose firm features and slight frown of intentness made a face of mark. A black-and-white portrait, plainly a bromide enlargement from the photograph below, hung on the opposite wall.

"I don't see why pa keeps his photograph up there," continued Mrs. Battles, her black eyes snapping, "mean as he's treated him, after he's bought goods there for ten years and paid prompt, too—much as telling pa he'd break him if he didn't pay up the note due this week!"

"Oh, ma, how can he pay?" cried Stella.

"He's mortgaged the building, that's how," returned Mrs. Battles, sombrely. "And he ain't left himself enough to pay the fire insurance."

"And pa's so scared of fire!"

"Well he may be; we was burned out once!" The woman sighed heavily. "I suppose I had ought to remember. Harcourt T. Wells was good then; but why did he want to turn on your pa *now?* Race couldn't do enough for that man. When we was married he was clerking for him; and he'd work overhours, and he'd turn his hand to anything for Harcourt T. Wells. Looked like he just revelled in doing for him; and he'd talk to me—why, you'd think the sun rose and set with him. And when he run for mayor, you remember your pa was fit to drop, he worked so hard. I ain't exaggerating to say your pa'd a-give his life for that man any hour of the day. Yes, he would, to-day. And look at the way he's been treated!"

"But he used to be kind once," Stella interceded. "I remember the things he sent, every Christmas!"

"He ain't kind, now. He hadn't got no business to fly out at pa like he done and pa not doing a thing. Jest for nothing but because he would give credit to the boys—those boys that always had traded with him. Your pa came home white as ashes. It was all I could do to get it out of him. He'd met Wells on the street walking with old Cochrane himself. Minute he seen your pa he twisted his eyebrows. 'Wait a minute, Mr. Battles,' says he—didn't call him Race, like he used to do, and looked like ice at him, and I know just how hot your pa got, for his collar was wilted clean down and it was a cool April day—'I hear you have gone back on what you promised me,' says he. 'I didn't promise you nothing,' says your pa. He told me he was kinder startled and didn't rightly know what he was saying. 'It was an implied promise,' says Wells; 'I advised you for your good. If you don't choose to follow my advice, well and good; but I warn you, here, I sha'n't take your bad accounts for any excuse next June. Good-morning.' And your pa, he was so dazed and so kinder wanting to cry, he felt so awful that he hadn't a word to say, just gasped like a fish out of water; and they walked away. It fairly made your pa sick. I never seen him look that way since little Harcourt died."

"He was named after Mr. Wells," said Stella, thoughtfully. "Ma, pa thought a great deal of Mr. Wells." She, too, now was looking at the picture across the threshold. She was trying to match this unknown feeling with her own friendships. She thought of her best friend at the High School; did grown men and women have their friendships, too? Such a thing seemed queer and almost indecorous, as vivid emotion of any kind in older people always looks to youth; but piercing her shamefaced, youthful estimation of her father's excess of feeling as not quite sensible, was a passionate thrill of sympathy.

Stella had her mother's limpid, long-lashed, dark eyes, and her silky, abundant dark hair, and her graceful shape was like her mother's at sixteen—indeed, at thirty, Martha Battles "kept her waist" and her beautiful arms—but Stella was her father's child. Martha took life on the broad side, laughing when she was merry, weeping when she was sad, and sputtering vigorously when she was in wrath. She was a true-hearted, loyal creature, and she made Race a good wife, and Race loved her with all his heart; but there were things impossible to say to his wife, that said themselves to his daughter. However, if Martha did not always understand her husband, she always admired him. To her, his short, thick-set figure was a model of manly strength; and the slouch in his shoulders (which in truth he acquired bending over the ledgers) was but the brand of a scholar. She had been a maid-of-all-work, and her father had shovelled on the street, and to her Race was a self-made man—a success that ought to be in the newspapers. There had been a notice of Race once in the Fairport *Blade*, and his picture; it was when he ran for alderman and was defeated. But everyone knew that there was no chance for his party in the ward, when he ran, and no mortal, unless it were his wife, had expected that the heavens would fall and his party's candidate be elected. The editor alluded to him as "the successful grocer and popular man, Horace Battles, Esquire." Mrs. Battles bought eight copies of the paper, seven of which she sent away. The eighth copy was laid in the leaves of the family Bible at the page recording the births of the children—only two, these were Stella's and that of the little boy who died. He had been named after Mr. Wells; and in the family Bible, after the line, "Died, May 13, 189—, aged 3 years, 5 months," in Race's handwriting, not so round and firm as usual, there lay on the page a sprig of dried lilies of the valley from the flowers which Wells had sent.

"Poor father," said Stella. It was the inadequate expression of a great many thoughts. In a moment she went on: "Now, ma, don't you say no, I'm not going to graduate. I'll let Bessie Page read my piece; and I'll get some good excuse so I won't be there. I'll write aunty about that place she said she could get for me for the summer, teaching those chil-

dren—the folks were to go away in June—
and I'll take it; and instead of being a drag
on pa, maybe I can help a little——"

Mrs. Battles had listened with quick intakes
of the breath, between a sob and a snort, but at
this last she exploded:

"Well, Stella Battles, do you think we're
going to let you go off as a nursery governess
when you've got a pa and a ma and a home,
and are the only chick or child we've got in
the world? And as for giving up graduating,
I won't hear of it. Why, I've been thinking
about it for a year, and putting aside money,
too; and your pa wouldn't take it neither; for
I did offer it to him to pay the insurance—
knowing how frightened he is of fire—and
says he, 'No, Mattie, no; it ain't enough for
that, and there ain't anything else on earth I'd
take it for. It's the only time she'll ever
graduate,' says your pa, ' and let her have the
good of it and look nice as the rest.' See here,
Stella, don't you begin to sniffle, there's your
pa this minute—be a-smiling!"

Mrs. Battles dressed her face in determined
radiance, as example, before she opened the
door. Battles came home by simply mounting the stairs, the grocery being in the floor

below. His daughter thought how light his footfall used to sound, and how his whistle of the last popular air always used to precede him. Now, the only sound was of a step that dragged. But he was trying to smile as he entered. Battles was a short, rotund, little man, who made his round face the rounder by two scraps of sandy whisker on his jaws. He wore these because Harcourt T. Wells, on whom as man and merchant he formed himself, always wore side-whiskers. He had a freckled face and very faint eyebrows and white teeth that flashed when he smiled, and his eyes were rather wide apart, giving an impression of open-heartedness and frankness. When he spoke, his voice was low and pleasantly modulated; but were he tickled into laughter, the mirth rolled out of him in loud, whole-souled peals. That day Stella wondered when she had heard her father laugh. She wished her mother had not said, " I've some good news for you, pa!" She caught the instant gleam of his eyes and the falling of his face at the end of the sentence; and although he kissed Stella most tenderly, and said, in the heartiest way, " That *is* good news; I'm proud of you, daughter; and how many in the class, twenty-five, mother? Well, well!" still Stella felt that the news he had hoped to hear was different. In a minute he added: "Wasn't that Mrs. Leroy I saw coming in here this morning? What did she say about the strike?"

"She said Leroy was coming in to see you this afternoon, but she wanted you not to say so to anyone. She said they had a meeting last night, but——"

"Did they declare the strike off?" asked Race, eagerly.

Mrs. Battles shook her head. "They voted Harry down. It was that Bellair. The men do be so taken with his talking!"

"Then there's no show of the strike's ending," said Battles. He gulped down something and drank his scalding hot coffee until the tears came; but he made so poor a pretence of eating that his wife cried at him presently, saying that he ate no more than a sparrow, and she was discouraged to cook.

"Well, I'm sick," said Race, his gloomy eyes on his saucer; "what I see makes me sick. Johnny O'Brien's baby died this morning, and Johnny made a kind of coffin for it out of some boxes I let him have. And

Rhodes gave him some white paint. To think of how Johnny used to set and talk about that baby. And he couldn't even buy it a casket! And the Wheelans, they ain't got shoes on their feet, and the Jenners have sold their cabinet organ; it makes me sick to stand there behind the counter and hear such things. Besides—I got an offer for the horse and wagon, and I guess I'll have to let them go." He was uneasily aware of the consternation on the women's faces in spite of his stare at his plate. He went on, desperately: " Nor that ain't all; I'll have to send Danny away."

"Oh, father!" cried Stella. "Poor Danny; he's so stupid he'll never get another job, and he's so willing and faithful."

"And what will his grandmother do, Horace Battles?" cried the wife.

"I don't know," said Race. "It's got to this, ma; we're like folks on a shipwreck, we're only trying to save ourselves. I can't raise even the $5 a week for Danny's wages; it's all I can do to pull through with my own skin whole. They do say that there's a car-load of new men coming; in that case the men will have to git out of town, and there ain't much chance of my collecting anything on the

"JOHNNY O'BRIEN'S BABY DIED THIS MORNING."

accounts, for, what with the expense of moving and all, they'll be all broke up, every mother's son of them. I don't see any way out!"

"Well, I guess we sha'n't starve!" said Mrs. Battles; "but that Swede family round the corner, they fairly ain't got enough to eat—and seven children under twelve—it's awful; I couldn't help sending them in some stew; I put in lots of potatoes and onion, and steamed over some hunks of bread, so the meat went a long way. Why, Race, those children glared at the dish—like wolves! I think that Bellair ought to be hung!" At the beginning of the fight it had been Cochrane to whom Mrs. Battles had wished a felon's doom; but the good woman changed front with an unruffled conscience, meaning only good-will toward her neighbors.

"I'm glad you took them in something. I wish you'd take the O'Briens in a bite, if you can fix it so they won't notice."

"You don't mean they are at that pass!"

"I don't know when any of us will get there," groaned Race, pushing back his chair and making for the door. But at the door he came back. "Don't think I ain't pleased and proud at what you've done, Stella," said he, his hand on her shoulder. " And it's a great comfort to know that come what may you've got your education."

" Oh, pa, I wish I could help you! " cried Stella, with a choke in her throat. He kissed her, but something in his own throat prevented his answering; and so he went heavily downstairs to the shop and Danny. The clerk was only a lumpish boy, at whom the customers were continually girding because he made so many mistakes; but he had a kind of dogged honesty and faithfulness that Race valued, and he was the sole support of an old grandmother, who prayed for the Battles, every day. Danny looked up at Race's step with the glimmer of a smile; he had cleaned the molasses corner and waited for the grocer's surprise. But Race did not see the humble offering of toil, he was plunging at his business.

"Danny, I got something to say to you," he began, as if primed for a reproof; and he ended with the bald statement that he should have to dismiss the lad at the week's end. It was a great relief to have Danny merely say, "Yes, sir. I know times are hard." But it was less of a relief to see the muscles of his neck moving as he hastily walked off, and to be sure that he had been crying when he returned. No one came into the store. Race looked out on the street and sat drearily conning over his own plight. His heart was like lead. He could look out and see the tidy little yards and the windswept macadam, and the men sitting idly on their steps for the most part, albeit a few were patching up their sheds or fences and some lawn-mowers were rattling through the little front yards. A stranger would have noticed only a pretty, shady street, but he saw the empty window where the Jenners's cabinet organ had stood, and he remembered how Ned Mueller had meant to paint the house which stood dingy brown and would wait a long time now for the paint-brush. He felt not only his own anxiety and pain but the smother of all the misery about him. A wagon dashed round the corner, a large truck drawn by two great Norman bays with shining harness. The letters on the side jumped at his eyes—"Harcourt T. Wells & Co." How many, many times had he watched wagons like those from the corner with almost the luxury of proprietorship. "Gittin' richer every day!" he would chuckle to himself; and plod along, beaming. Now his heart contracted at the sight, and at the feeling that he no longer could exult in Wells's grandeur as in something part his own. Wells had been the grocer's hero, worshipped from his business principles to his whiskers. The times when Battles would call to pay for his groceries were proud moments to him. He would saunter into the great store, nodding here and there to the clerks, who all knew him, and ask, in a careless voice, "Old man in?"— just as if he had not chosen the hour of the day most likely to see Wells in his office. Then he would pass the card of "No Admittance," cocking his eye at it as he passed, and trusting that there might be some stranger present to view his confident entry, and walk up to the head of the firm's desk with "Well, here I am again, Mr. Wells." It was a standing joke that Wells should say, "After an extension, Race, I suppose?" and he should answer, "After a receipt in full, I guess." They always both laughed, and then would follow a chat of a few moments. Mr. Wells's opinions on matters of political moment were sure to get the best circulation in Race's giving. "Well, I was talking with Harcourt T. Wells and he said," etc. Thus would the words of the oracle be repeated over Race's counter. Wells having no honorary title—a secret grief to his admirer—Race always gave him his name in full; it was never "Wells" or "Mr. Wells" but always "Harcourt T. Wells." It goes without saying that Wells's politics were Race's. That he should ever oppose Harcourt T. Wells was a catastrophe too awful for the follower's imagination to compass. And here he was in the thick of it. "But I *couldn't* do no different!" groaned Race, sinking his head on his hard palms, "I couldn't go back on the boys!"

Henry Leroy, president of the Fairport Labor Congress and foreman in the foundry of the Cochrane Plough Company, was Race's familiar friend. The men in the works were mostly his neighbors and customers, good neighbors and good customers. Where was he to look for custom were he to drive them away? And he had the acuter form of sympathy which springs from eye-knowledge. It is one thing to read in the papers that strikers are suffering, quite another to see the sewing-machine of the Spriggs's trundled down the steps, and to watch Dick Spriggs's wife (who always sent a plate over when she fried doughnuts) go back with her apron to her eyes; or to hear Johnny O'Brien, who used to be full to weariness of funny stories about his baby, begging the street commissioner for work on the sewer that he might pay for the baby's funeral. Race not only knew what decent, industrious fellows many of the Cochrane men were, he knew how, all winter, the wages had been pared and pared until the men were fretted into a panic, seeing no end. He had heard in Swedish, German, and Irish dialects all about the obnoxious new "bosses" and the new rules and the petty oppressions, born quite as much of ignorance as tyranny. The grievances that pick men's pockets and the grievances that nettle their pride—Race got them all, struggling meanwhile to overquell prejudice and resentment with appeals to prudence and "the women folks and the kids," and mild reminders of the tough old Scotsman's good qualities. Now, condemning the precipitation of the strike, he could not help a sympathy for the strikers. Wells, on the other hand, only saw the immediate subject of conflict, (which, in fact, was puerile), and the hard con-

HE HAD HEARD IN SWEDISH, GERMAN, AND IRISH DIALECTS ALL ABOUT THE OBNOXIOUS NEW "BOSSES."

ditions of business making a reduction of wages inevitable. He wanted Race to join with the other tradesmen in refusing credit to the strikers and thus " knock the strike flat." Race did promise to see the butchers and grocers. But he found them firm for the strikers. So, wretchedly enough, he went to report his failure. Wells was out of town. To write a letter on anything more delicate than the price of groceries was a stupendous matter to honest Race. " I'll wait and see the old man, and explain," said he, mopping at the wrinkles fast settling in his forehead. Wherefore it fell out that Race's patron received his first news from the paper friendly to the strikers. And it was Race's hard fate to run up against Wells and Cochrane at the climax of Wells's explanation how his trustiest henchman had deserted him. " Oh, I'll answer for Battles; Battles is all right! " he had assured Cochrane; and here he must confess that Battles was all wrong. Race's appearance gave a ready opportunity to release his anger and disappointment. Nor did Race, an afterwitted fellow at the best, find a word of reply. He stumbled away like a fool, and so the trouble began. And yesterday, when he

paid Wells, paid him every last cent due—and
it was like drawing blood to raise that money
—when he came into the store thinking, anyhow, he'd get a good word from him, then
what happened? They told him Mr. Wells
was busy, and would he wait? By —— he
wouldn't wait; he said it was no consequence,
he only came to pay some money—and he paid
it, every cent! There wasn't enough left for
the insurance on the house; and fire was the
dread of his life. "I wouldn't have minded
so much, if he'd spoke to me, himself! I'll be
broke up fast enough; ain't he satisfied with
that?" groaned Race. It did not distract him
from his dejection—although the act had that
intention—to go to the door and look about
him. What a comfort just looking at that
building had been to Horace Battles! "To
think of me owning a handsome brick store
like that!" he used to muse in a glow of deli-
cious wonderment. Every one admired the
building, three stories high, narrow to be sure,
but of generous depth, with a large, arched
window, and a high, dark-green panelled door,
and fixtures and woodwork of a beautiful
cherry-red; a store so shining clean, so sunny,
and so tasteful in summer (when a tiny foun-

tain played amid radishes, lettuce, and strawberries) that strangers often craned their necks backward as they were driven past the neat gilt sign. To-day the windows were quite as clean, but the display was dismally meagre. The dizzy pyramids of tinned goods in their gray papers had dwindled to two towers of fly-specked cans of pease. Danny had tried to eke out the tableau by a barricade of soap and a row of bottles containing an unsuccessful, though deserving, brand of pickles.

Farther down the street the grimy brick walls of the great plough shops turned their blank windows and barred doors sullenly on the little homes that used to light their household fires at those smokeless chimneys. Two watchmen paced languidly in the sunshine, an unconscious compliment to Leroy's discipline, else would their heads have been broken long ago. Leroy himself came up the street. He greeted the watchmen in a matter-of-fact way, saying something that Race was not close enough to hear; but he saw that each of the men eyed the labor leader's back; and they spoke together.

Leroy was a tall man, muscular and cleanly built, with an ease of motion often seen in those whose muscles are kept in trim by exercise. He wore his brown curls short, and a firm chin was clean-shaven, but his mouth was hidden by a mustache. If his mouth had the expression of his eyes, it was very gentle.

"Well," he said, "Race, I couldn't wait until evening."

"What's up?" said Race; "you boys going to give up the strike?" Leroy shook his head. He followed Race into the store, where Danny was arranging the shelves and futilely trying to fill the gaps with decorations in the shape of placards. The boy's eyes were red. Leroy nodded to him and went on to the tiny office. He balanced himself on a stool by the desk, and absently printed Race's stamp on a card flaunting the purity of Royal Baking Powder.

"How did it go, Harry?" said Race, to start him.

"All wrong. We're beat, and the longer we keep this up the worse we're beat! I'd have got out of town last month but for seeing the boys through."

"But, Harry, won't they take you back?"

"Not they. There's the disadvantage of

being president; I try to hold the men back, in the first place, and get their ill-will as a pusillanimous——"

"But they know better now!"

"Some of them, not all by a long chalk, or they'd back out of the strike. And the company thinks that I egged the men on. I'll not get taken on, no matter who is, you can bet your life on that!"

"But you're such a good workman!"

"Good workman doesn't count. They think I'm a meddler, and stirred up this racket to further my own ambitious purposes. God knows what *they* were, *I* don't. But that's the way it goes. The union always catches it; and the union leaders are always to blame; and yet from my experience, I'd say that in nine cases out of ten the leaders are for peace and prudence, and prevent more strikes than they cause, ten to one. When they do go into a strike it's either because they see no other way to prevent the men's being ground to powder, or because there's a crazy pressure on them from the hot-heads that they can't resist. But you don't hear of the strikes that are prevented; and when a strike does come off, you see the officers' names in the paper and they're making the speeches; and when a fight begins, even a fight you're opposed to, it ain't in human nature not to sail in and put up the best fight you can! But that isn't what I came to talk about. My goose is cooked. Well, I made a living before I ever saw Alan Cochrane, and I guess I can make a living without. But here's what I'm after. There is always a lot of outside sympathizers who like to be in any muss going, and they keep the hot-heads stirred up; and as things go from bad to worse, the sober fellows catch the fever; *they* want to swipe somebody. There's a lot of bad blood in town, a lot, Race. You know there's talk that Cochrane's going to bring in a carload of new men; and these crazy fellows are swearing that if that's so the new men sha'n't find any shops to go into. May be all talk, but it's ugly talk. I don't like it; and I sent a note to Cochrane offering to send some men to guard the shops. He declined. Said as much as that I had something cloaked by the offer. It was," said Leroy, his mild voice deepening a little, "It was a pretty insulting letter. I warned him to keep away from the shops, nights; but he's sandy as the devil and he goes just the same. Perhaps if you were to see him and tell him what I'll tell you, he might take it as corroborating me, and be a mite carefuller."

"Well, I call that real forgiving of you, Harry, helping Cochrane out of the hole this way!"

Leroy's calm brown eyes blazed suddenly as he answered with a novel heat, "I don't give a d—— for Alan Cochrane! I wouldn't cross the street to save his immortal soul! But I won't have any dirt charged up against the union while I'm bossing the fight! It's those cussed fools like Dick Bellair and Raney and Brown that *kill* a strike! They act so, no decent folks can sympathize with the strikers! D—— 'em!"

"That's right," agreed Race. "Hullo, there's my little girl! How'd you get home so early, daughter?"

Stella's figure in the door-way, with the sunshine behind her, was so brightsome a picture, in her pretty print frock and broad hat trimmed with roses, with the flush on her delicate cheek and the light in her soft eyes, that it might set any father's heart to a lighter measure. With all his worries, Race smiled.

"Can't I see you for just a minute, pa?

Will you excuse me, Mr. Leroy?" said Stella, her pretty manner the prettier for the girlish blush that came with the words.

Race went a little apart with her, rather puzzled. It was not like Stella to run in on the business. Stella held "business" in proper awe. But she could hardly wait now to have him well out of eat-shot. Hastily she held out her hand and showed him some bank-notes. "There's $15, pa," she said, breathlessly; "it's ma's and a little I had saved; and ma's willing; we talked it over, and we couldn't sleep nights if you turned Danny off. *Please* take it, pa; it'll pay three weeks' wages, and *lots* of things may happen in three weeks! Please, pa!"

"And the graduation dress and ——"

But she interrupted him: "I don't need the dress. I'm going to leave before we graduate. Ma's willing."

Race stood silent, his eyes filling with tears. How he felt he could hardly have told himself. He only was sure that he could neither take the sacrifice nor refuse it. In the pause Danny, on the other side of the partition, slunk away with his knuckles in his eyes. "Daughter," said Race, finally, "you wait;

THE SEWING-MACHINE OF SPRIGGS'S TRUNDLED DOWN THE STEPS.

I'll think it over. Maybe—maybe I won't need to take your money to keep Danny. You wait. No, you needn't leave the money with me."

Leroy himself turned away then and walked to the door of the shop, where presently Battles joined him.

"Now," said Leroy, not looking at his friend, "I'll tell you what I've found out."

. . . .

Alan Cochrane's house stands no great distance from the plough works. He is an elderly Scotchman, a widower these twenty years, with no nearer kin than his seventh cousin, Mrs. Graham, who keeps his house, and he cares not a pin's head for fashion. His big, square, wooden house, stands in its large, old-fashioned garden, as it has stood for twenty-five years; although, long since, its neighbors have been transmuted into shops or storehouses, or have been razed to the ground to make room for brick walls. The blinds in front are always closed; why, only Mrs. Graham can tell; it is her custom as it is her custom to wear black silk mitts and to allow no followers to her maids—wherefore she often is left with no maids at all.

When Leroy and Battles came to the iron gate (a high iron fence enclosing a hedge surrounds the place) Leroy paused. "I'll not go in with you," he began, but he took a quick step backward in the shade of the hedge, darting a warning frown and beckoning to Race to do the same, which Race did mechanically.

"Why, Harry," says he, "there's five of those fellers going up the steps. What does it mean?"

"It means, I guess, that they're smarter'n I counted on their being, and they're going to catch him at home where he won't have a soul but women in call; and it's Thursday, the cook's day out; and the meeting-day of the Presbyterian sewing society that Mrs. Graham goes to regular as taxes." He was looking the whole street over while he spoke, not seeing a soul in view. "I guess you and I will have to tackle this job, Battles," said he.

"Sure," says Race. "How'll we git in, Harry?"

"Easy; they've got Raney's cousin here; she knows me and I've got their password. See how she'll give me the glad hand."

Race knew the girl himself, having in

pleasanter days often handed her the family flour and berries, and she smiled in a frightened way on him. Leroy had not touched the bell; he had only knocked in a peculiar fashion. She had instantly responded.

"All right," said Leroy, very low; he added another word.

"You're sure *you're* to come, too?" said the girl, who seemed scared out of her wits. "Oh, I'm sorry you're in it, you and Mr. Battles."

"Never you mind *us!*" said Leroy, kindly, but always in the same low voice. "We'll help and not hinder."

"Don't let 'em hurt him, will you, Mr. Leroy?"

"I'll try my best," returned Leroy, rather grimly.

The two men stole down a dark hall, through what appeared to be a dining-room, and took breath outside a heavy black-walnut door. Race's pulses were drumming, but Leroy looked as pale, dejected, and calm as usual. He slid his hand back to his hip-pocket. "Yours all right?" said he. Race nodded, imitating the motion.

"Then, listen!"

Cochrane's voice came to them distinctly. "No, I won't sign an agreement to take you all back at half the increase, or *any* increase, or take you back at all; and you won't kill me without a fight!"

Leroy laid his hand on the door-knob. His lips formed an inaudible whistle. He stepped softly across the room.

"Look out of the window," he whispered.

"The window's open," reported Race, "but there's a screen in it. There's a balcony outside and we could swing ourselves over and batter the screen down with a chair or something."

Cochrane had stepped back, edging nearer the library-table and the drawer where lay a revolver; and young Billy Mooney (the reckless one of the crowd, half drunk and only eighteen, which is an age of the Evil One's own picking does it come to wicked deeds) was making between when the screen crashed forward and Leroy bounded into the room, Race close after him.

"Don't fire!" he called to Cochrane; "we're on your side."

"Which side?" cried a big fellow with a red face; "which side, Harry? D—— it, we're in earnest. He's going to sign, by ——, or we'll make a vacancy in the firm!"

"Hardly," said Leroy. "Get your revolver" (to Cochrane, who needed no prompting but flashed it out of the drawer). "Brown, I warned you fellers I wouldn't have no dirt, and I *won't!* It ain't five to one now, but five to three — and the telephone! The police will be here inside ten minutes." The man nearest the door quietly slipped back the bolt.

"Are you going to go back on the boys and fight for the scrubs, Harry?" cried Brown.

"I ain't going to let you disgrace honest men who fight fair," said Leroy, firmly. "Time's short—are you going to skip or wait to be pinched, while you're parleyvooing?"

"If we do go now," grumbled another man, "we'll be pinched before night anyhow. I'm for doing up the whole——"

He stopped; there was something clammy and ugly in the impact of Leroy's revolver jammed against his shirt-front.

"Get out, and you may save your skins for all the informing I shall do," said Cochrane, who had been taking in the whole scene with an ironic smile. "But I advise ye, lads, to skip out of town; the sooner the better."

"Who gave us away, Harry?" said the big man—the others had unostentatiously sidled to the door.

"That's my lookout," said Leroy.

The big man made no answer, although he turned on Race a glance of menace. The youngest of the party relieved their chafed vanity by a few threats; but in the end, and no long time either, they left the three men standing together.

"Will they be setting the house afire going out, for a parting token, do ye think?" panted Cochrane.

"They are more likely to pay Race or me that compliment," said Leroy, quietly.

Cochrane wiped his brow. He was a portly man and he was puffing with his exertions. "I'll buy me a bicycle, this same day," cried he. "I must work down to fighting weight; those blackguards would have done me up if you hadn't come in so handily. Well, will ye take something?"

"I never drink, Mr. Cochrane," said Leroy, coldly; and Race, with more courtesy, declined the proffered decanter.

Cochrane chuckled under his stumpy gray mustache. "Weel, at least ye'll let me thank

ye. Those fellows were primed for murder, no less. They had juist enough speerits in them to be wicked. I see ye were right in your caution, Leroy." He held out his hand, but Leroy turned red and took a step backward, saying, very stiffly, " You owe me no thanks, and I owe you none, Mr. Cochrane."

Again Cochrane chuckled. " But ye got the police? "

" No, sir, I didn't. That was just a bluff. Battles was coming to warn you, and I was only going to the gate with him, when I caught a glimpse of Brown and Raney and the others, and of course I went in. There wasn't a cop in a mile! "

" Weel, ye did the bluff fine. Man, ye'll shake hands. You're a man and I'm a man; am I no? And we've fought together. It's no the preesident of the Cochrane Plough Company, or the chairman of the Strike Committee; it's juist Alan Cochrane and Harry Leroy—eh, Battles? "

" That's right, sir," said Race.

" And I may as weel tell ye," said Cochrane, " that's all a lie about the carload of new men." (Leroy's eyes flashed.) " And if the union send you I'll see ye to-morrow, and we'll talk it out. If you'll come back at the old wages they'll not be cut, and in a month or two I'll be able to raise them a bit; and the other things we'll talk over. Ye can all come back; there'll be no discreemination, not even against them "—jerking his thumb at the window; " they'll most like be running anyhow, the fule bodies!"

" I'll do my best, sir," said Leroy, in a different tone.

" He's done his best against the strike all along," Race put in.

" Only because I thought the strike had no chance of winning," said Leroy, stiffening again.

Cochrane's sharp little gray eyes twinkled. " Losh, man, don't be scared that I'm putting ye on my side. Ye'll let me think ye an honest enemy, will ye no? I'll conseeder those same grievances."

This time it was Leroy's hand that was extended first. " Then, good-afternoon, and I'm glad I came, sir," said he, shaking hands, as he would shake hands with the great political personages to whom he was sometimes presented when there was need of the labor vote. Race followed his example, observing the same form.

"For the matter of that, I'm glad, too," said the old Scotchman, dryly.

Returning, Leroy was in higher spirits than Race. The non-combatant ruefully considered how he, who only wished for peace, had now fought on both sides, to his own proper loss and peril. Having angered his best friend past forgiving by helping the strikers, he had now won the ill will of the most reckless strikers by fighting for the hated Cochrane. The baleful eyeblink shot at him by Brown rankled like a poisoned arrow. He thought of Cochrane's speech about fire, and Leroy's answer.

"And me with not a cent insurance," he groaned; "but, Lord! they wouldn't be such fiends!"

Were they? It is past telling. No clews were found. The five suspected men were full of pity and innocence from the teeth outward. Alibis were ready at hand for every one of them. Nor is it sure that they were not genuine, these alibis. A defective flue, the unpunishable incendiary in so many cases, may have played its tragic part again. Whatever the cause, this at least is certain, Race's building, grocery and home, was burned that same night. The fire-bells awakened Harcourt T.

Wells, a bachelor, lodging in a hotel. He counted the strokes—half the numeral in bed, half out on the floor scrambling into his clothes—for it was Cochrane's number. That was enough to send him downstairs to the telephone, and the sleepy answer, " No, it's not Cochrane's, some grocery, Battles's, they said!" spurred him hot foot through the streets. There is something in a midnight fire that pricks the nerves. It may be the contrast between the quiet streets outside, with the dim stores, the shrouded counters, the shadows of the tall façades on the roadway, the white porcupines of light blinking and winking in the dark, violet air, and the seething excitement that waits around the corner. Or it may be that the touch of pathos in human calamity and the touch of horror in human peril blend with a shuddering appreciation of the pageantry of the sight. The meanest structure flaming in the night, borrows a ghastly and sinister beauty. And more than anything, it may be that fire-bells, especially fire-bells in the unguarded hour of darkness, startle the imagination with the sympathy of a common dread; to-night, you; to-morrow night, we, perhaps! As Wells pounded down the sidewalk, he could hear the thud of his own footfall; and he remembered another time of his hearing the same sound, the time when his own great store was afire—then, Race and he were the last men on the roof!

Snatches of many scenes drifted through his mind, in which one humble, faithful figure stood, as if against that red glow in the west; while he ran, heedless of his years and his weight, faster and faster. All he had heard from Cochrane that afternoon, all he had heard in Race's store before he went to Cochrane's, made a mingle-mangle in his brain, like a tune to his hurrying feet.

First he passed a black mass of heads. Then he stepped over the line of hose and found a crowd of Cochrane's men, every man of them carrying something that he had pulled out of the smoke. Cochrane was on an empty box, directing the loading of some drays; and swearing and shouting at the men with as much fervor as if nothing had occurred to disturb their relations; the men themselves running and tugging with the heartiest obedience. The building was masked in smoke. It poured from the windows. The firemen were fighting the fire on the roof; and the wing in the rear was blazing. Wells ran to the front, where was a heap of household goods not yet removed, although Leroy was busy with a score of helpers. Half a dozen loudly sympathizing women were grouped about Mrs. Battles, who sat in the wicker arm-chair on the best hair mattress, rocking to and fro, unconscious of an extraordinary toilet of her best black silk skirt and Race's trousers flung hastily about her night gear, in mistake for a jacket, and Race's Sunday silk tile perched on her woful head; equally unconscious that she was huddling two photographs, the bust of Clytie and the bust of Abraham Lincoln, to her breast.

"Where's Race?" she wailed; "where's Race Battles? Danny, where's the master?"

Soot and flour had made a grizzly charcoal study of Danny as he tottered up to her, crooked by a huge white sack. "It's the very last sack of flour," gasped Danny. "He ain't inside. I was all over."

Mrs. Battles screamed. She could see her husband. He was on the peak of the roof, apart from the firemen; and he held the garden-hose in his hand.

"Hush, ma, don't be scared," said Stella.

"RACE, YOU OLD FOOL, COME DOWN!"

The girl was dressed and calm. "See, they're all coming down!"

"But *he* ain't!" shrieked the wife; "he's staying. Race! *Race!* Come down! Let the store go! What's the store to me if you get killed? Race! Come this minute! Oh, he can't hear me. Mr. Wells, *you* call him; he'll mind *you!*"

Then Wells did a reckless thing. He, Harcourt Wells, no longer a young man, elbowed the women aside and ran up the ladder like a foolhasty boy.

"Race, you old fool, come down!" he bellowed. The roof was smoking. The firemen were gone, safe down off the other ladders. Race stood alone. He faced the smoke volleying toward him, spitting burning cinders from out the glare behind the murk. His white shirt was puffed out by the wind of the fire, and his face was like the shirt, as he trained his poor little squirt-gun of a hose on the crackling roar.

"My life's insured but the building ain't," he shouted back; "I've *got* to save it."

Swearing roundly, Wells stumbled up the roof. "I'll *pull* you off if you won't come!" he howled through the din. He grabbed

Race's leg. Race dropped the hose; and he did turn now.

"You're crazy," he cried. "Get off, for God's sake!"

"Crazy yourself!" snapped Wells. "Here, you get down that ladder first, and find your wife."

They slid down together. None too soon, either, since the roof whereon Race had stood crashed in before their feet touched the ground. Race felt Wells's hand on his arm hauling him back. He clung to it, piteously shaken, and began to laugh. "You ain't mad at me—that's most worth the fire," he quavered.

"Of course I'm not mad at you, you blooming idiot," growled Wells, who was puffing and perspiring at every pore as well as burned by a dozen cinders; "why in thunder didn't you come round and give me a chance to say so? I wasn't going to take your money the other day; I knew how it squeezed you. But you wouldn't wait a minute. No, you must needs go off half-cock! You needn't be looking so black and blue, either. I came around here to-day and saw your clerk, who isn't such a fool as he looks, and he told me all about the insurance and the little girl's being willing to give up her dress and all. *I* paid the insurance policy, Race, this afternoon. You'll be a year or two to the bad, but I'll see you through. And the little girl shall have as pretty a frock at the show as any girl in town —Cochrane and I'll see to that— D—— it, Race! you aren't hurt, are you? Here! Somebody! Get some whiskey!"

"It's—it's only just the smoke. It got into my windpipe, I guess," sobbed Race, the tears running down his cheeks. "Smoke's terrible on the eyes. God bless you, Harcourt T. Wells—it's only just the smoke!"

THE WAY OF AN ELECTION

THE WAY OF AN ELECTION

IT was a special-delivery letter, and Leroy, after he had receipted for it and the boy's red wheel was twinkling down the street, eyed the superscription a moment before he took out his pocket-knife and very neatly opened the envelope.

The time was five o'clock of a Saturday afternoon. The foreman in the foundry at Cochrane's always came home earlier Saturdays, the whistle blowing release at four. Harry had come up on the cars, and was resting a moment on his piazza before cleaning himself for supper. He was tired with a hard, warm, dirty day's work; and he waited a moment in a pleasant daze, conscious of the splash of the improvised hose fountain on the green plush of the tiny lawn, of the rich colors of the cannas in the pyramid near the house, of the shifting of the burnished greens of the oak-trees under a light breeze, of the soft blending and melting of many hues in the angles made on either hand by the shady street before him, of the flowers and shrubs in the yards and the fanciful architecture of the wooden houses, of the rattle of passing vehicles over the brick pavement, and the noiseless flash of bicycles. The Leroys owned their house, a new house, painted cream color, with gables and a large piazza. They were very proud of the house. Years had been spent planning it. There were as many as three large closets, and a garret, and a bath-room, upstairs. When Harry used to emerge from the cleansing ministrations of that temple of tidiness, he felt that now, indeed, he was living in luxury and that the grime of the foundry was a trivial thing. Harry, his wife and their three children, had watched the hewing of the joists and admired the mortising. They thought few carpenters could have turned such beautiful round pillars, or so dexterously beaded the piazza railing; and the sunburst carved over the north gable assured Mrs. Leroy that their dwelling was not merely a house but a mansion.

"I do wish Jay would come and see it," she would say twenty times a month. She never added, "Now, maybe, he'll be willing to stay with us!" She never distinctly said it to herself; that were to reflect on Jay's affection; Jay, who was so amiable to the children and often brought her a pretty trifle from Chicago and always praised the cooking, although he lived in a hotel in Chicago, where they had icecream every day for dinner. Yet the unavowed perception of his discomfort over their humble conditions, moved beneath the current of her thoughts like an undertow. It sailed openly through Harry's thoughts. But he never showed it to his wife, not even when Jay borrowed money of him for his hotel bill. He lent the money silently, only telling himself that it were cheaper for him did Jay come to his own house. "Oh, well, I must put up with his foolishness, Effie's so fond of him," he said, tolerantly. Jay was Effie's only brother, younger than she; and she had stinted herself, all her youth, to earn him the education that she felt his abilities deserved. He was a young Chicago lawyer and politician now, whose fluent speech and fine clothes filled his sister with a pride that she tried to believe satisfied all her hopes. He bowed to people in Fairport that she only knew by name, and talked familiarly of all the great ones in her little world. And once, at a political meeting, she saw him on the platform among the vice-presidents, in his black frock coat and white tie, stroking his mustache and smiling, quite at home. It was a glorious moment. Possibly Harry was not so happy; but he loved his wife, and he had been a good friend to Jay.

Being so good a friend—a friend in need, one may say—he did not like the looks of his brother-in-law's hand on a special delivery envelope. He frowned. "I hope Jay ain't in a scrape again!" he muttered, with an uneasy quaking of his pulses. Then he unfolded the sheet and read; and the color drifted out of his bronzed face, for this is what he read:

"HARRY: I guess you will think I am a scoundrel; but I was dead frozen sure that I had a sure tip on a wheat deal, and if I'd won out we would all have been rich, for I meant to do the generous thing by Effie. But I was fooled. I had to put up margins you know, and I had raised all I could, and they wouldn't take my note without your endorsement. Now a man that used to be a friend of mine, but has quarrelled with me on politics, is out gunning for me, and has got that note, and it is likely he will send it to your town for collection, as it is due to-day. I believe the d——scoundrel suspects. Harry, it's the penitentiary, no less. Harry, if you let me be arrested, I swear I will blow my brains out. But if you will save me *this once* I will never forget it as long as I live! And I will pay you up certain sure, and pay the other money you have lent me, too. *Every cent!* There's another thing. I know R—— well. I've filled him up with your great influence with the workingmen. Both States are so confoundedly close this year that the managers are opening their hearts. They are willing to plank down $2,000 for your campaign expenses (between ourselves they won't be anything to speak of) if you will do your best for us, on both sides the river. Now, Harry, the note is only $1,342; so if you accept you will have the money to meet it, in hand. And it's sure; they will pay half in advance, and half in November. Don't leave me in the hole, old man, for God's sake! It would break Effie's heart. Burn this. J——."

Leroy sat perfectly still for a few minutes. His face continued to grow paler. Suddenly the tide turned in his heart. He clinched his fists and crumpled the letter in them, while the blood began to color his cheeks and forehead until they were a dull, painful red.

His first distinct thought came as a bicycle glided athwart his vision and the child on it touched his little cap to him. He thought, "I can't get Tommy his bike—or me one, either." He laughed: an American always laughs when he gets a sudden blow. "The $600 in the bank will have to go. And—I guess I'll have to put a mortgage on the house. I thought it so awful fine when I got the other paid off. Well, it will be more natural with one on. Oh, Lord!"

His patient face contracted. "If this was the first time," he muttered, "or if I could be sure it would be the last!" Drearily his memory took up the squalid roll of Jay's "troubles." Jay had been grateful after each escape; and came the more easily at the next peril.

It was somehow wretchedly nagging to remember Jay well dressed, jocose, lightly pushing his misdemeanors behind him. "He to say I ought to get Effie a wheel like his "— somehow Harry harped on this one string of his grievances—" when I got her a good

LEROY SAT PERFECTLY STILL FOR A FEW MINUTES.

wheel, a pretty wheel that was ten dollars more than she thought I was going to pay! D—— his airs!"

"Hullo, Harry!" a man called to him. The man carried a tin dinner-pail and a carpenter's kit. "You going to the meeting to-night? Big meeting. Darcy's going to talk."

"Politics, I suppose," said Harry.

"Yes, he'll skin the Shylocks alive. Better come. Darcy was wonderful the last time I heard him."

Then Harry felt the same rush of blood at his heart which he had felt before; but, this time, he did not repel the thought instinctively; he said: "All right, I don't mind hearing what you fellows have to say."

"That's right," said the other, evidently pleased. "You can answer if you want to, you know."

He walked off, humming a tune.

Darcy was a smart fellow; Harry was not so sure as he would like to be, that he was honest. He did not agree with him on the question that was in everybody's mind; he himself had been studying it for months in the laborious, thorough-going, workingman's fashion. He had talked it over with his comrades at the shops; with Race Battles, the grocer, who had given him a very fair abstract of Mr. Harcourt T. Wells's economical reasoning; with Cochrane, and with Alderman McGinnis; slowly, his opinions had hardened. But he had held his tongue. Now, suppose Jay and his friends were right. A great many people believed that they were right; and that the triumph of their party would make poor people rich. Just suppose they were; he could easily—he hadn't committed himself to any party—well, where was the harm in hearing Darcy?

He shook his head and went upstairs to his bath and his Saturday-night toilet. His wife fancied that he was rather absent-minded at supper; but he was gentle as always.

After supper (and during the meal he couldn't help speculating whether they needed to have both eggs and meat at the same time; and how ever he should explain the need of minute frugalities to Effie without lying) he went down town. He thought of riding; but withdrew his foot from the step of the car. "I'm getting extravagant," said he. The same reflection made him replace his tobacco-bag in his pocket.

The hall was a bare room, up two flights of stairs. It was already filled with men, most of whom came in their working clothes. There were so many dark flannel shirts that the room wore a dismal air in spite of the raw white walls and the flaring gas-jets. Most of the men were smoking, and an odor of stale beer, from the saloon below, mingled with the tobacco-smoke. A shout greeted Leroy's appearance.

He had never been there before.

"I only came to see what you fellows would make out of it!" said he, brushing the jubilant congratulations and welcomes aside. "Oh, they all say that," he heard. "Just listen to Darcy!" "I'll listen," said Leroy, "but I've been reading and thinking a good while, and I am more than half of the opinion——"

"Yes? Yes?" cried two or three at once.

"I'm more than half of the opinion that you fellows haven't a leg to stand on!"

"Aw, come off," cried the most eager man, yet not angrily; it was plain that Leroy was a great favorite.

"I've knowed Harry to be right six times,"

said another man, " and I ain't knowed him to be wrong once."

" Well, that's a record."

" Jest let him listen to Darcy! " cried the first speaker; " Darcy is the boy! "

Leroy sat as if he did not hear; but it was quickly passing through his consciousness, like a vibration to that first thrill of gratified vanity, that there were other men with whom his words would have equal weight. Suppose what the one party were continually declaring should be true, and the defeat of their cause meant cruel hard times for workingmen, as well as paralysis of the industries of the country, and national dishonor, what would those who had followed him over the precipice have the right to say to him? He listened without interest to the early speakers, men who had not yet learned to marshal their ideas in connected and effective speech. One of them was a man in his own shop, a good worker, but slow and unready; he never would get any higher wages than he got now; he was growing old; he had a great family and a sickly wife. " I don't know what's the matter, boys," he mumbled, for he had not many teeth, " I know I've worked hard for forty-two years, ever since I was a boy of ten, and it does look like things is gittin' harder every year."

"Wages aren't. They're higher!" called Leroy.

"And things to eat is cheaper!" called the man who had known Harry to be right six times. He had a loud, cheerful voice, and a cheerful young face with many freckles.

"I ain't denying it; but times is harder," reiterated the speaker, turning his dim and anxious eyes on Leroy. "I tell you, gentlemen, we're ground under by the money power, that's what's the trouble. I got ten children myself——"

"That ain't the fault of the money power," observed the irrepressible, cheerful man.

"And I had to borry fifteen dollars last May, and I had to give a morgige on my wife's sewing-machine, and I've been paying ten per cent. a month on that, one hundred and twenty per cent. a year. What do you think of that? I ain't got it all paid yit. I tell you, boys, I'm willing to vote *any* way to stop them kind of things."

He sat down amid applause and cries, "It's a shame!" "That's right!" "Down with

Shylock!" Two or three of the light-minded, however, were calling sonorously on "Dick!" "Dick Williams!" "Dicky boy!" The cheerful man (*he* was Dick Williams) was whispering eagerly in Leroy's ear.

"Wait for Darcy," said Leroy. But while the next man rambled through the "crimes" of the opposite party, by the aid of notes, which he could not always read—in these intervals of embarrassing study being encouraged by Dick, with a shout of "Louder! louder!"—Leroy set his teeth and thought. He was thinking what hard times mean to laboring men. He did not need to imagine, he had only to remember. The drops were pricking his brow. He was roused by frantic cheers. Darcy had risen.

Quietly he stood, his hand in the breast of his coat, waiting for the applause to subside. He was slim, pale, with wavy black hair and melancholy black eyes. He wore a slender black mustache, his face otherwise being clean shaven. He was neatly, almost foppishly dressed, and his hands, in particular, were most carefully kept. They were very white. As he talked he moved easily about, and his gestures, even in his most impassioned

THE MEETING.

moments, never became grotesque or violent. "Darcy never tries to scoop up the planks of the floor!" Dick Williams expressed it. His chief oratorical charm, however, was his voice, a beautiful, magnetic organ that could deepen without growing harsh, and ring without flattening on its highest notes. His tones floated, sweet, full, and thrilling into the silent listener's ears. He began very quietly. He gave the ordinary arguments of his political creed, but with a deft and fanciful turning of his own. Then he sympathized with the old man who had spoken, describing his honesty and industry so warmly that his subject was between grins and sobs; from him Darcy fell upon an undefined and rather hazy "money power" with such vehemence and glowing metaphors that the hearers yelled and shrieked their delight. But honest Dick, after a sharp poring over his hero's face, observed, dryly, "Big talk; but say, where do *we* come in?"

Harry shook his head. His heart sank within him like a waterlogged boat. He had come to be convinced, to hear logic, facts, what he himself called "the horse sense of the situation." What he heard was a hash of exaggeration and falsehood, gilded platitudes, hysterical wrenchings at the emotions, and frantic appeals to the wolfish prejudices of class against class. But how magnificently the orator acted his sorry part! Convincing himself with his own molten passion! Swaying himself and his audience in the same breath!

"I call upon you to rebuke these Shylocks who eat the poor as it were bread!" he shouted; "I might—so powerfully have my feelings been stirred by our friend's simple, pathetic story of his wrongs—I might ask you to tear their luxurious roofs from the heads of these bloodsucking plutocrats; but I believe in the ballot. Crush them, but crush them beneath the avalanche of the American freeman which comes down upon the tyrants and their tools as white, as noiseless, and as irresistible as the storm king of the Alpine hills!"

While the room was ringing Harry arose. And honest Dick choked and clinched his fists in his nervousness. No one could help contrasting the two men. Leroy's tall shoulders stooped a little. His figure showed muscular strength and the ease of it; but it had no touch of Darcy's supple grace. His hands were large and hard with handling hot iron. They looked strong, not shapely. He did not seem "magnetic." He had a patient, kindly, firm face, kindling now into earnestness.

"I only want to say one word, boys; I'm not going to make a speech. Mr. Darcy has been talking to you of 'the money power'—what is the money power?" (A voice, "The banks.") "The banks have to get their money somewhere: who gives it to them? (A voice, "The rich men.") "The rich men and the poor men, too. I have been round to every bank in town, inquiring into these sort of things, for I like to be sure I am right before I go ahead. (Applause—mainly from Dick Williams.) Boys, the bulk of the savings-bank deposits and some of the other deposits come from poor people and people of small means. I tell you the money power is just the people—the rich and the poor together. And I tell you what's more, that the banks are not oppressing the people: they lend money from $10 up; I have borrowed it; I know plenty of men have borrowed it at eight, and seven, and six per cent. a year. McCann's story made my blood boil; but what's the money power got to do with that—what does Darcy want to bust the banks wide open for on

account of that? *He* never borrowed the
money of a bank; he borrowed it of a little,
dirty, private usurer. I ain't in no avalanche
business myself, but I'll go over to that robber
to-morrow with Mac and his receipts, and I'll
get the money that he ought to have back for
him! (Great laughter and applause, led vigorously by Dick Williams.) So don't vote for
his party, for it wouldn't punish him a little
bit, since he isn't a banker; he is old Jack Fanning, who is——" An immense uproar took
the words off his tongue. Fists and open hands
were waving in the air; and half a dozen fiery
patriots were demanding, "Did he lend you
the money? Did he? Did he?" of the bewildered McCann.

"Yes, he did, gentlemen," faltered Mc-
Cann; "but I didn't know he belonged to *us!*"

"Very likely not," said Leroy, coolly;
"and you don't know a good many other
things any better. Before you boys decide to
turn the country upside down you better find
out whether you ain't jumping on the wrong
people just as you were this time."

"That's right!" bellowed Dick. And as
Leroy sat down he added, "Last car's coming.
Move we adjourn."

"Headed off that time," he chuckled, as the crowd poured into the quiet street under the white electric light; "say, Harry, don't you be afraid, the boys know you're white and they'll stand by you."

"And I'll stand by them, the best I know, Dick; the best for them, whether it's the best for me or not."

"That's right," said Dick, easily; but he wondered a little at Leroy's unusual, almost oppressive, solemnity of manner. "Folks do get awful worked up with politics," reflected he; "but if that Darcy tries any of his slick, fake talk on Harry, and makes him feel bad, d—— if I don't knock his flannel mouth off him! Good job, too."

This same evening, for hours, two men had been sitting in a private parlor of the principal hotel of the city. The table before them was strewn with letters, clippings from papers, and railway maps. Now, although a full hour later than the adjournment of the meeting that had been momentous to Leroy, they were still sitting, still talking. The tall man with the gray, curly hair and the indefinable, well-groomed air of an Eastern club man, was a great national politician. The other man, shorter, slighter, and younger by ten years, was quite as careful in his dress and his beautiful hands; but he was a local politician. He was very rich, very respectable, very much in earnest; he was in politics because he was a citizen who had opinions, not because he wanted an office. At this moment he looked worried. "I don't like the looks of the thing; it looks— well, it *doesn't* look like a legitimate campaign expense. Do we absolutely need Darcy?"

"We do," answered the national man, flicking his cigar-ash, with a patient smile, like one willing to go over the same ground unnumbered times; "to say nothing of his Labor paper, he has a wonderful hold on his audiences, McGinnis says."

"McGinnis is the most cheerfully venal politician I know."

"My dear Colonel, who denies it? But he is perfectly honest with his employer—after he has taken his side and his campaign bank account is all right. And he is working like a beaver."

"Maybe," admitted the other, wearily; "he does seem interested. After all, I think it's the decent, honest men that make me the sickest—too timid to speak out, too lazy to go to primaries, and too d—— stingy to give a cent to campaign funds. They seem to think that their whole civic duty is performed if they go to the polls once a year. It is enough to make a man want to emigrate!"

"Or reconcile him to the McGinnises. Hullo! That's his knock—Come in!"

The door softly, one might say insidiously, swung inward, admitting a large man in a fresh white duck suit, to which a florid face and a pink silk shirt gave a pleasing dash of color, further emphasized by glossy black hair and a black mustache. He was as much more aggressive, pictorially, than a blond man in the same clothes as a colored lithograph is more aggressive than a water-color.

He greeted both gentlemen with a certain deference, not common to Michael McGinnis. The local magnate (in spite of his criticisms) returned a smile of good-fellowship and the national man a flattering cordiality.

"Well," was his first inquiry, "do you bring news, McGinnis? How about Leroy? You still think him important?"

"I do that, sir. There isn't a man more respected in the unions and out than Leroy. You see, they know he's white—honest, you know."

"How would we best get him? If he were offered——"

"Excuse *me*—you know him, Colonel, he wouldn't handle any money. There's only one way to catch Harry."

"And that?"

"That is, convince him the election of your platform and your men will really help the laboring man, and you've got him; he'll swallow you all, hook, line, and sinker! I'll tell you 'bout Harry. I had a letter from a good friend of mine in Chicago; he's on the other side, but they've done him dirt, and he ain't dying to have them win, though he's regular and he's committed and can't say anything openly. See? Well, he told me that he knew for sure that Harry Leroy got an offer of $2,000. We're the storm centre and we're two sides of the river, two doubtful States at once—oh, they want us bad!"

"Well," said the national politician, "will he decline?"

"Will Joe Patchen beat a scrub?" McGinnis opened his arms in a fine swinging gesture.

"He *has* declined. He gave 'em the marble heart. This evening he declared himself. He's been studying and thinking. No good to press him. Meself, I've supplied him with literature. Well, to-night there was a meeting of the Jefferson Club. Darcy he was there, and so was Leroy, and so was a nice boy I know, Dick Williams. I thought it worth waiting for his report." Therewith McGinnis gave the details of Leroy's speech with much humor.

"He *is* a good fellow," said the national man; "but, now, about Darcy. You think we still need him?"

"Sure. You get Darcy rigged out with a stereopticon and pictures showing the workman to-day and how he'd be if they was to win, and have a picture to show the mortgage being foreclosed and that sort of thing. And tell 'em who has brought on the hard times; and show 'em how much harder the times will be if those fellers get an innings. Give 'em the figures right in their own county. Tell 'em about the way mortgages will be foreclosed with *them!* That hits 'em in the neck. Say, I got a little chap, kin look over the records and get the facts pat for him."

"But will the other fellows go out to the lectures? You know they've passed the word down the line not to attend our meetings."

McGinnis showed a flashing set of teeth. "They kin pass the word till it's worn out, but in the country they'll cram the school-houses for a free show like that. And if Darcy gets 'em in front of him with them facts, and his own eloquence and a jolly lot of campaign songs for the local talent to sing—why, don't you see, it would be *great!*"

"I see the advantages," said the national man, dryly; "but how about Darcy? he's committed to the other side——"

"I know," said McGinnis, with a sigh; "we'll have to put up a good deal more dough."

"It's merely a question of that with him?"

"Just that. Ye see, he ain't got the money yet; he's dickering with them. And their offer is all in the air, while ours is——"

"Spot cash," said the national statesman, dryly.

McGinnis permitted himself a frank grin. "'Tis as I expected. Well, gentlemen, we got Leroy, we got him for nothing. Now, 'tis agreed we want Darcy?"

"I suppose we have to have him, d—— him!" groaned the respectable local statesman. "When can you get him?" said the national man.

McGinnis edged his big thumbs into the armholes of his coat. He shed a radiant Celtic smile on the two politicians, thence he flung it up to the portraits of the candidates of a great party, which had been thoughtfully tacked on the wall.

"I *have* got him," said he; "I got him to-night."

The national chairman laughed outright.

"Colonel," said he, suavely, "you are next the bell, do you mind touching it? They have a choice article of fizz stowed away here; I am not willing to drink Mr. McGinnis's health in anything less."

"Aw, come off!" cried McGinnis, in bashful delight, blushing with pleasure; and his blush deepened as the local man cleared his brow and joined in the laugh, saying, "Well, there's no question, McGinnis, but you're a man of action. Did you—eh—ah—name any figure for his campaign expenses?"

"No, only intimated I knew they would be large, put 'em a notch higher than the other fellers' notion. 'Besides,' says I, 'you want to be on the winning side. Now, I'm inside and I know we stand to win: I know what the canvassers report; I'm betting two to one on us.'"

"Actually, Mike?" said the national man; he had never called him Mike before. McGinnis hoped that the bell-boy, who was at the door to receive the order, heard that one word, as the door opened.

He waited until it closed on the boy. "I am," said he, then; "I never was surer. If we can git Darcy we can throw enough extra votes right here to help us out with two States. I bet a thousand dollars this week, and I'm a poor man—comparatively," he supplemented, with a grin.

"Well, I'm glad to hear you talk that way," said the local man; "take another cigar." He proffered his own case instead of the box on the table.

McGinnis took his triumph modestly; but it warmed his soul. He had risen from the ward to the county; he had won innumerable victories first on the spoils side, lately—such are the amazing alliances and vicissitudes of politics—on the side of honesty and reform;

but never before had he felt himself within the mystic circle where the game is empire and the stake the destinies of a nation. He had never been so happy since poor Polly McGinnis, to whom was reared the most splendid and tasteless monument in Saint Margaret's Cemetery, promised to be his wife; and suddenly his heart softened with a tender pain—if only he had Polly to tell it all to, how these great gentlemen treated him and called him Mike. He felt so much that his florid skin lost a shade of its glow; and he sat very quiet until begged to " go on."

" Well, he was a good deal impressed. ' I suppose you folks are spending money like water,' says he, thoughtful like. ' Well, we ain't mean,' says I. Then I gave it to him straight, he would git more from us than from the others. And I outlined the campaign. He was tickled with the stereopticon and campaign-song notion, I could see that! ' Now,' I says, ' you're a labor leader, and you know, all nonsense aside, honest injun, labor ain't got nothing to gain and everything to lose from this new fool ruction; come on and help the real friends of the workingman for once!' Well, he begun on Harry Leroy and consistency, and that rot; jest his vanity, of course. But I cut right in. 'I know what Harry said about Fanning; it's true, too, and it's true about the money power, and how your fellers winning will affect the poor man. Ain't it? Ain't you going to be impressed and kinder haunted, and ain't you going to look up things more to down him than anything; and ain't you going to be appalled, simply appalled by what you find? And ain't you after what will help the workingman; and it don't cut no ice with you whether folks call you inconsistent or not—you *want* to be inconsistent when you're in the wrong. And you've come to the conclusion them fellers have made the hard times they complain of themselves; they've held up the country, and now you ain't in favor of electing the robbers to the police force.' That's how I gave it to him, and he tumbled to it like a gentle bird. 'McGinnis,' he says, ' you're great! ' So he's all right."

" And you brought them both down in one night?" said the national man.

" Well, I don't claim any credit for Harry. I only lent him books. It's because he's white he's with us; but I did take the liberty of asking him to come around here to-night. It's a

HE TUMBLED TO IT LIKE A GENTLE BIRD.

good night, being Saturday; and I'd like real well to have you gentlemen see Harry and give him a kind word. After all, it's all he'll git."

"Is he downstairs now?" asked the national man. "We'll be glad to see him; he'll take the taste of Darcy out of our mouths a little."

"Well," deprecated McGinnis, "Darcy's down there, too—in a private room."

The national man smiled grimly while the local man opened the door to admit a bell-boy with two silver buckets, piled high with ice from which rose a refreshing stream of coolness. The national man motioned him to another room; and McGinnis gleefully commented to Michael, "He won't drink with everybody; bet he have Darcy in first." Which, indeed, proved to be the case.

The interview was not long; McGinnis acted as master of ceremonies; the national man went directly to the point—the local man was communing with the ice-buckets in the other room.

"Mr. Darcy," said the great politician, "Mr. McGinnis tells me that you are good enough to be willing to help us not only with your paper the—ah—*Hammer*, but in the campaign. I'm very glad to find you with us."

"I have refused an offer of two thousand, sir, and my travelling expenses to stump for the other side," said Darcy, firmly, and McGinnis solemnly nodded.

"That's good," said the national man, smiling, "for you see that is precisely what *we* want you to do! You know Mr. McGinnis's idea?"

Darcy said that he had heard some details; it was a great idea, but—there would be large expenses.

The national man, who had been jotting down figures rapidly on a sheet of hotel paper, pushed it over to Darcy. "That's my estimate. It may come to a little less or a little more; call it that and you take the lump sum. McGinnis will attend to the statistician and the lantern, etc.—separately. If the arrangement is satisfactory I can give you half now and the other half the day after election. I'll make out a memorandum which you can sign."

Darcy's brilliant eyes flashed as they saw the figures. His black brows met, however, when he read the "memorandum," passed first to McGinnis, and receiving a glance of heartfelt admiration from that astute practical politician; but he affixed his signature in silence; and the gleam returned to his eye as the national man offered a roll of bank-notes. " Will you count it? " said the national man; " one makes mistakes occasionally. Thanks." He repeated the sum in his crisp, Eastern accent. " Do you know, Mr. Darcy, I fancy you are going to set the prairies afire. You should hear our friend McGinnis talk about you! "

" Well, you've got me hard and fast, gentlemen," said Darcy, with a dry glance at the receipt which the national man was stowing away in a silver-rimmed lizard-skin pocketbook, " but I believe your cause is right; and it will have the best efforts of my heart and mind. I'll get out on the road as soon as we can get the other things in shape."

" A cigar, Mr. Darcy? " said the national man, politely; and again Mr. McGinnis inwardly grinned; it was the box and not the cigar-case that was offered. " Won't you come in some time to-morrow? We are to have a little conference of the workers. They will all be glad to see you." He shook Darcy's proffered hand, or, it would be exact to say, he allowed Darcy to shake his hand, and bade him farewell with much politeness.

"Don't he carry it off well!" said McGinnis, the instant the door closed behind the orator's figure; "well, that's one kind of a labor leader, let's see the other."

"Yes, you get him, and we'll get out the buckets," said the national man. And his greeting to Leroy and the talk which followed not only made Leroy wonder in his modest soul, but further convinced McGinnis that the great politician understood human nature without a key. "Talked right out before Harry and me, both of them, like we was on the ground floor. Hully gee, Michael, but you are just *there*, and don't you forget it."

He felt, somehow, a sensation of gratitude to Leroy, a new respect as he heard his own opinion asked. He had used the same device in smaller matters, many a time; but he experienced a simple kind of pleasure now that it was used toward him; he felt at the same time the flattery of the subtle distinction between the politician's manner to Darcy and to his present auditors. He treated them like political equals. Verily, it was a proud and happy evening to Michael McGinnis. Leroy barely lifted his glass to his lips; he never drank; but Michael did the champagne full justice. Michael's head was strong, he was not in the least dizzy when they shook hands warmly with the great men and went out of the hotel, together; but perhaps before those—Heaven forbid I should betray confidence, I being an unseen spectator, and give the definite, cruel number of glasses!—before the champagne, let us say, he might not have hummed so cheerily,

> "Then Ireland shall be free,
> From the centre to the sea,
> Says the Shan van Voght,"

or encircled Harry Leroy's neck so fraternally with his arm as they sauntered down the lonely, lighted street.

Harry smiled; but in a second, the vulture that had been clawing at his heart all the evening, and that had relaxed its grip for the hour, under the stress of higher interests, tore him anew. Involuntarily he sighed. McGinnis's eyes flashed. "Say, Harry," said he, looking amiably at the electric lights, "I had a mighty funny thing happen to me to-day; I was down your way, and I saw a little special-delivery boy—I got him the place, he lives in the Eighth Ward—and he was scorching along to your house and nearly ran into me. I asked him where he was going, after I had said what was proper for his conduct—we've got to have a bike law in this place, that's sure as death! He told me your house, and showed me the letter. I recognized Jay's hand. Fact is, I had news of Jay this very day, and I suspected that he would be writing you; that's why I questioned the boy. I—I guess"—McGinnis dropped his arm and linked it in Harry's— "I guess Jay told you about that note."

"How—" began Harry and stopped, uncertain what he should say.

"How'd I *know?*" said McGinnis. "Well, fact is, Harry, I met Meecham, and I bought that note."

"It's endorsed by me," said Harry, huskily; "I'll pay you, Mac."

"Naw, you won't. Jay Sibley will pay that note. He'll pay every last cent. Not jest this minnit, but as the money comes in. I'll handle that young man without gloves for his soul's good. He ain't *my* brother-in-law! Don't you lose a mite of sleep, Harry. I'll fix him and there won't be no scandal or bad

"I'M ONE OF YOUR CONVERTS."

times. It'll all come right in the wash. You just say you've seen me, or, better still, you don't say nothing at all. *I'll* write him; and when he comes up here, you'll see a very much reformed and penitent young man. Here's your street-car, Harry—that's all right."

He had pushed Harry and his broken thanks onto the platform as he spoke.

. . . .

A month later Leroy met Darcy, both being on their wheels. "Well, Darcy, how goes it?" called Harry, with a cordiality that he had not felt for years; "I hear you are doing *grand work.*"

Darcy's wheel was shining and beautiful; Harry's was a second-hand, rattling machine of a make unknown to fame; but probably not a man in town had had more pleasure in riding than he. He looked tanned and happy.

"That you, Harry? how well you ride! Why, things seem to be coming our way all the time. But I feel as if I wanted to tell them all—I have told a good many, that I'm one of *your* converts, a brand snatched from the burning, as it were. I was switching off on the other tack when you set me thinking—that evening at the club, you remember—about old Fanning. I began to look things up, and I was appalled, simply appalled at what I found out."

"I've read your speeches," interrupted Harry, "they are full of argument, facts——"

"Yes, when I came to look things up, I found there was only one ground for me to take, and I took it. I want to be right, and this talk of consistency doesn't cut any ice with me. I hope you get the *Hammer* all right. Say, I hear you're doing a lot of work right along."

"The best thing I ever did was to convert you," said Harry, laughing; "I never could quite take that story into camp until now, and felt I was getting credit under false colors; but now I shall 'point with pride'— Well, good luck to you, and let me know if I can help you any time."

As he rode along, he thought, half wistfully, but without a grain of envy, "I wish I had that man's talent!"

Darcy smiled to himself, watching him. "He's dead easy," he muttered; then, all of a sudden, with the swift transitions of his temperament, he bit back a sigh.

"D—— it!" he almost groaned, "I wish I had that man's conscience!"

THE
MOMENT OF CLEAR VISION

THE
MOMENT OF CLEAR VISION

THE gas-jet flared unsheltered above Thompson's head, painting the silhouettes of three men on the white plastered wall. Thompson's had an eagle nose and pointed beard (which tilted in the air, as he talked); the other two had each a mustache and a good, firm jaw. The three men were members of the Labor Council, although belonging to different trades. Thompson was a printer. He had been a drinking man, inclined to riot in his cups; but it was an open secret that Harry Leroy had made a reformed man of him; and now he merely smoked and swore to excess, and was on the best terms with the police force. The other two were hard-headed, conservative, skilful workmen of the class that does the most for the unions while needing them the least. The man with the heavy mustache was a carpenter, the man with the scanty flaxen mustache was a rougher in a steel mill.

All three were smoking, all three wore a troubled air, which in Thompson's case was tinctured with irritation.

"Yes," said the carpenter, "the boys decided to keep on with the strike. Going to appeal to the Council to help 'em. That throws it all on us. If we say we'll support the strike, why, they'll keep it up; but if Harry can hold the Council back, there is a lot of conservative fellows, married men, you know, that'll be only too glad of a chance to take what's offered."

"They were offered about everything that they struck for, seems to me," Thompson grunted between puffs; "extra hour on Saturday, grinders got the rise they asked, and they promise to take on more men, so the fellers Haverly bounced can all get back."

"*Will* he take 'em back, though?" said the steel-worker, "he used 'em cruel rough; I guess he's made the strike, and 'long's he's there no man who has dared to stand up to him will feel safe. And they ain't going to give in about discharging him, you bet! That's the way. Nine times out of ten, in strikes, it's some fool boss makes the row; and then the firm, instead of giving him his walking papers, stand up and fight for him—'cause it's discipline. That was the way at Homestead. That was the way at Pullman. And that's it here."

"That's right," said the carpenter, "you don't catch me doing a turn in the Hollister Plough Works while Ike Haverly is Superintendent; and all the other concessions don't go while he stays."

"But he ain't going to stay," said Thompson, impatiently; "they won't discharge him under fire, that's true enough; but while you boys have been shouting and parading and howling at Harry because he won't let you boycott the other companies doing business with Hollister's, he's been quietly working and making sympathy for you and seeing folks that can talk up to Hollister; and Harry told me that Haverly's got another job offered him and he's going to take it. Next month. Harry says so."

Both listeners showed excitement. The carpenter whistled. "That ought to fetch 'em. Harry's a good 'un. But—will they receive a committee from the Union and see West when he comes? Say West and Harry, West for the Unions, and Harry for the Labor Council?"

"Nit. That's where Hollister says he'll fight as long as he's got one brick left on another in his factory. He admits Haverly was in the wrong and the men have had grievances. He's willing to redress them; he'll see all the committees from his own men they want to send; but he won't see outsiders. That he swears."

"That's where they'll split, then," the steel man sighed. "West is as stiff as Hollister. He'll come down to-morrow night; and if he makes one of his razzle-dazzle speeches to the Council there'll be no holding the boys. They'll be for endorsing the strike, making an assessment, having a boycott, and anything else the hotheads ask."

"He ain't got half the sense in his speeches Harry has," snarled Thompson.

"Maybe," admitted the steel man, "maybe. Harry's pretty clear, and he talks sense every time; but the trouble with Harry is, he ain't got no magnetism. And West is chock full of it. He gits them to shouting before they know it. It's the easiest thing in the world, I do believe, to make men do fool things. There's nothing tremendously exciting about sense—in fact, it's kinder dampening, usually; but you can make an awful fine speech about the way the laboring man is ground under by the Shylocks and the tyrants and the soulless corporations, and goading and prodding them! Besides, Victor knows lots of poetry and big words, while Harry's speeches—why, you can understand every blamed word Harry says."

"I *want* to understand!" said Thompson.

"So do I; but it ain't so grand. But the main thing against Harry is, he ain't fiery enough; he's all for law and order. If you knocked him down, I guess he wouldn't do more than call the police!"

"That's all you know of Harry—hush up, that's his knock!"

Thompson flung back the door and Leroy entered, mild, gentle, gravely courteous as usual. Even Thompson, looking at him, listening to his leisurely tones of greeting, swallowed a sigh. "I *wish* he didn't have that underdog look about him," thought Thompson.

"I've got something to propose to you, boys," said Leroy.

Victor West sat, cramped and stifled, in the

stuffy chair-car and gazed out of the rigid storm-windows that had been screwed into their winter position to repress lawless ventilation. The yellow kerosene flames swayed in the aisles, and the darkening landscape without was no more than a blur of trees and plain.

"I suppose the brakeman will call the place," thought West, "and anyhow Leroy telegraphed that he would be on two or three stations before. I wonder if he thinks he can move me." His lip curled; he had the impetuous nature's contempt for the moderate, cautious man. Leroy had seemed to him (during the two times of their meeting) to be timid and slow. "He can only do a retail business in anything," was West's notion; "probably he is not a physical coward, but he is scared of anything big, strikes or anything else. I must stir the boys up."

He laid his head back against the soiled red plush; and the light showed how pale was the skin, how sharply cut the delicate features. Many a rough man had looked up at that haggard face and those burning brown eyes with a swelling of the heart. West had a charm; even his enemies admitted that. There was a sweetness in his boyish radiance of hope, his

"I'VE GOT SOMETHING TO PROPOSE TO YOU, BOYS," SAID LEROY.

frankness, his eager cordiality to those of his own party; and no one in his company for half an hour, could resist the assurance that he was absolutely sincere. While he rested, he was going over the heads of his speech. Argument, invective, appeal thronged tumultuously into his mind, to be dressed by every resource of his wit, and fancy, and passionate faith in his cause. At last, with a sigh of relief, he opened his eyes and muttered to himself, " Yes, that ought to fix them! "

Just at this moment the train jarred and moaned itself into a stop. The vast purr of the engine throbbed in his ears, pierced by a voice at his elbow. " Excuse me, Mr. West? "

West sprang up and made room for the newcomer to sit beside him. Leroy was the same neutral tinted, phlegmatic soul as ever, he decided—look at him now parting his coat-tails carefully as he sat; neatly arranging his overcoat across his knees; and trying to smooth the pocket-flaps over something that bulged out the pocket. What a Miss Betty he was! And such a fellow thought that he could fight *him!*

Victor was not conscious of vanity; considering everything, he was not especially vain; but the image of slow, stupid, moderate Harry Leroy, expecting to overquell his brilliant self, struck him as funny. And yet his sensitive nerves felt an attraction in Leroy. And he had a curious kind of pity for his sure defeat. He began the conversation in a kindly strain. Leroy went to the point at once. He told his story. They had really won everything for which they were fighting. Why not accept the terms offered and everybody go back to work?

"How about the Union?" said West, "will they meet us? Will they recognize the Unions?"

"They won't discriminate against any union man; they won't promise not to employ non-union labor; but as a matter of fact about all the men do belong."

"Will they let you and me, or any of the Labor Council meet them, or do they demand that the members of the committee they see shall be their own men?"

"They want them to be their own men, but they may belong to any union. I understand the point you would make; but I think we are risking the bone running after the dog that took it. If we go in now we shall get what we

THE MOMENT OF CLEAR VISION 93

are fighting for; if we stick it out for a point like that we shall lose the public sympathy, and the firm will gain it; and feeling will get bad. It has been a very decent strike so far. The firm hasn't tried to get in new men. But they will if we stick it out; and that means the devil of a time. I don't think we ought to risk it."

"But for a principle," said West, with his pleading smile. "I hate a strike; but what are a dozen strikes if we win a principle like that? We must make them recognize organized labor."

"A lost strike ain't going to help us."

"Ah, but we sha'n't lose it; and if we do, it will be after such a fight that they may be ruined men, or pretty near it."

"I'm hanged if I see how Hollister's men are going to be helped by ruining Hollister. In that case, they are out of a job for good and all."

"Someone else will take the factory; and you may be sure that he will not be so ready to fight labor."

"Do you think it is so easy to sell factories? It may be six months, may be a year, may be *never*, and the men have got to live meanwhile; there are their meat and grocery bills going on all the while, and their children's feet wearing through the shoes. You talk easily of ruin, but an employer's ruin ain't no fun to the men he employs."

Something in his tone nettled West; it conveyed to him a biting idea that Leroy thought him young and crude, and unbusinesslike. Because business was West's weak side he was the prouder of his capacity therein, and the more ready to flare up at any criticism. He swallowed his chagrin, but it rankled within him.

"I am not underestimating the hardships of the men in this strike; but you must remember I have to look out for not only them, but for labor in general. Individual hardships must be borne for the sake of the cause."

"If the cause is worth it; but it ain't worth keeping decent, honest, hard-working men awake nights just to get a blazing triumph for the leaders in this strike, and that's what it comes to."

West reddened; but Leroy checked the words on his lips by a gesture, while he continued: "I know you're only thinking of the real welfare of workingmen. So'm I, Mr.

West. I know you don't care for any personal glory, or victory, or any of that slush. You want the men to be the better, not the worse for this strike. And so do I. Say, can't we get together, somehow, and save these boys? They've spent all their money, and they're running up bills. They know they haven't got a chance if the Council don't help 'em out; but if the Council backs them up the hot heads will win out and we'll all be in the mire together. We'll have to be assessed; and if, as is likely, they ask a boycott on Hollister, then all the firms that have any dealings with him will be pulled into the muss. Here we are at Cochrane's, for example; we're getting along all right, we've no kick coming. Cochrane is a square man; I tell you in confidence, he's helped a deal to get this proposition from Hollister; but he ain't going to throw his friends overboard at any union's dictation; and before we know we would be walking out ourselves! You see the situation?"

"I see what you mean, Mr. Leroy," said West, stiffly, "but I am obliged to differ."

Then they went over the whole ground again. This time, in the sleeper, where (as Leroy said) they could talk without interesting the men in front and behind them—and have some fresh air. Leroy paid for the seats. As West noted him fumbling in a lank pocket-book for a fifty-cent piece not too readily found, he remembered that Leroy had contributed more than anyone to the strike fund; and his secret irritation at the conservative man's criticism softened; almost, he felt a moving of sympathy for the slow, stupid, timorous, honest fellow. He explained his position with courtesy, in fact with gentleness. Nevertheless Leroy was not so obtuse that he did not perceive that his words were wasted. He looked intently at West, whose pale cheeks were flushed, and whose eyes sparkled as he talked. "You put your side well," he said, "I hadn't much hope I could make you see things differently. But—I'm sorry." He nodded his head so dismally West had to straighten his lips.

"Here we are," Leroy continued; and he motioned to the porter coming for the bag, "no, we don't want to be brushed." But he slipped a dime into the man's hand.

Before they were well on the platform the train was speeding its lights away.

"It's not so large a town as I expected,"

said West, blinking in the semi-darkness, and looking down the one long, dimly lighted street visible; " where are the boys? "

No one stood about the little shed that served for a station; a single shabby carriage was drawn up to the platform.

" There's the hack," said Leroy, " the boys must have thought the train would be late— it never is on time, scarcely—and stepped over to Ball's to get a glass of beer while they were waiting; I guess you'd better go in, while I stir them up. I'm sorry—this way, Mr. West."

West had no suspicions, although the reception struck him as cool, and he did not half like it. He got into the carriage, a weather-beaten country " hack," politely reassuring Leroy. It was undoubtedly all right, the committee would hear the train, and the carriage was there, which was the main thing. Leroy jumped in beside him.

" We'd best look 'em up, I guess," said he, while the horses, which a glance had told West were better than the vehicle, plunged off at a gallop.

" Are they running away? " cried West when Leroy had righted him, for he had tumbled across the seat at the start. Still he did not suspect; he took Leroy's answer for what it seemed.

"No, they're just a little fresh, that's all."

But when the breakneck speed continued with no check, and no sign of excitement on the box, a snake-like fear squirmed into West's consciousness.

Thought was not much quicker than his action, which was to grab the handle of the door. Instantly his arms were gripped from behind and Leroy's voice was in his ears, as pensive and drawling as before, yet, be it his imagination or not, informed with a sinister resolve, "Be still! Keep quiet and you sha'n't be hurt; but if you try to get out, I'll have to hurt you."

"See here, this is kidnapping; let me go!"

"Better not try!"

The tussle was strong but short. West was no match for the moulder's muscles, and he sank back exhausted. Not a word had been said. "I suppose you'd shoot me rather than let me go?" he sneered.

"I'd hate to do that," said Leroy, gently.

There was a quality of such inflexible resolution in his tones that West felt a thrill crawl down his spine.

"Is it Harry Leroy, who made such speeches for law and order, talking?" he exclaimed. "What do you expect? What good will this do you? You can't mean——"

"I don't mean any harm to you, but I do mean you sha'n't go to the meeting and stir up a row to-night. I've thought this all out. I've got a pair of handcuffs in my pocket and if you won't be quiet I'm plenty strong enough to put them on you. And I will."

"It's all a plot, is it? I suppose luring me into the Pullman was part of it."

"They don't call out the stations, there," said Harry.

"And I'm nowhere near Fairport or the Mississippi?"

"Not very near," said Leroy, rattling up the ragged shade.

Prairie, nothing but prairie, dun and dark under the stars, sweeping off in darker ploughed fields or lightening in the glistening yellow-gray stubble of shorn corn, and devouring shadows streaming ahead of their lamps and their horses' flying hoofs. The lights of the town were gone; he could not put his head

out the window to find them. West began to
feel a disagreeable, gooseflesh feeling. He re-
called divers stories that he had slurred over
lightly in the past—" The men had been
carried away by their natural and righteous
indignation; they misunderstood and went too
far "—was that the damfool way he had talked
himself? He knew better now. There was no
safety in these appeals to the brute court of
last resort, to-day his side, to-morrow it might
be clean against him. He had not hated those
things enough. They were all wrong. But
Leroy couldn't be meaning to do him a mis-
chief—he had been seen with him, the conductor knew him—did he, though? Wasn't the
reckless daring of Leroy's plan perhaps its best
chance? Curse his own stupidity! The argument was only a trap. And he had let this
fellow whom he despised entrap him! He
could have torn his hair, but for the childish-
ness of it. He did grind his teeth. Leroy
never offered a word. They sped on, now
splashing through mud and now rolling
smoothly over the elastic turf.

West's fevered brain kept a whirl as rapid
as the horses' hoofs. A new spectre flaunted
before him. He might be kept in captivity

and released drugged, with hideous slanders about him that would ruin him. He had from a sneerer at Leroy become willing to fear almost anything from his dare-devil cunning. His mind went back to his speech, whereupon involuntarily he groaned.

"I'm sorry to disturb you so much," said Leroy's soft accents, "but I take it it's better one man should suffer than four or five hundred, and maybe a great many more."

West disdained to answer, so spent was he with his unavailing wrestle and his fury that he was afraid, indeed, that his voice might break. Silence fell between them and lasted a long while. The horses' lope changed into a good, round trot that did not slacken until they jolted over the rails of an electric road, and West saw the glimmer from a car flood the seat and Leroy's features, a second, before it faded. The horses broke into their gallop again. In what seemed a half hour to West (but he was aware he was not likely to compute time accurately) the coachman silently pulled them up. The carriage stopped, and Leroy, raising his own window, whistled twice. The whistle was answered by a number of whistles in different keys.

"All right," said Leroy, "we stop here. If you don't resist or try to skip, no harm will be offered you. Please get out."

The coachman had extinguished the lanterns. By the starlight the forms of two men were dimly outlined in the shadow of the lilac bushes before a gate. West opened the door. He expected them to take him by the arm. They did not move, but he heard Leroy's footfall on the gravel behind him. In front, at the end of a winter-stung garden of mingled flowers and vegetables, such as one meets in the Western farming country, was a two-story wooden cottage, painted some dark color, with the usual piazza and a withered vine clinging to the light pillars. The lower rooms of the cottage were lighted, but the shades were closely drawn. West thought of Dr. Cronin and the death-trap in Chicago. He halted. At the same instant he heard the noise of a carriage driving rapidly away, and, turning his head, he saw the swaying back of their "hack" as it jolted over the prairie.

"Please go on," said Leroy.

West walked up to the house in spite of himself, but at the piazza he stopped. "If you are going to murder me you can do it outdoors!"

Those were the words on his tongue, but they never were spoken, because, even as his hands clinched and his lips parted for them, the door was swung open, and a voice cried, heartily, "Come in, Vi; what are you waiting for?"

West's heart gave a great jump of relief. Mighty well did he know that tall, square-shouldered shape, that bald head with grizzled curls about it, and those honest, twinkling gray eyes; and even better he knew the thin little woman behind, whose still comely features were palpitating with good-will.

Instantly he was wringing the man's hard hand, and reaching his free hand to the woman.

Why, he even knew the rag carpet on the floor and the Rogers group of "Weighing the Baby" that stood on a familiar marble-topped table in the corner.

"Why, Uncle Phil Smith!" he cried, "Aunt Maggie, is this really you?"

"It's us both, Vi," answered the man, "sorry and glad, both, to see you this minute; will you go to the kitchen sink to wash your hands like you used to, or go upstairs to your room? Supper'll be ready soon's you are."

West, bewildered, turned his head to find Leroy. Leroy was not in the room. The door was shut.

"It's locked, Vi," said Smith, quietly, "locked outside. And those shadows on the winder curtains, them's men. I hope you won't try to get out, Vi; it would only make you trouble."

"Where's Leroy?"

"He's had to go back to town, by the 'lectric cars, to catch the next train for Fairport, so's he can speak in a meeting they have to-night."

"And you would keep me a prisoner here! Uncle Phil, I didn't think that of you, I did not."

"I got to do it, Vi," said Smith, quietly.

"Besides, he thinks it right to do it; and so do I," Mrs. Smith added. "Pa and I don't want those poor boys to keep up the strike any mor'n Harry does. Nor you wouldn't neither if you knew as much as Harry does about things; but I told Harry just how set you could be, for all you were the sweetest-tempered and kindest boy I ever knew except— except my Hughey!"

Her voice changed on the last word and she

turned abruptly; and the man's eyes followed her as she went out of the room.

West gasped. He did not know as much as Harry Leroy! And Mrs. Smith, who had been almost a worshipper, to tell him! But he answered, civilly. "You don't realize the danger you're in. This is nothing better than kidnapping. I can have Henry Leroy arrested the minute I get to Fairport. It's against the law. I can send him to the pen!"

"You'd have to send us, too, then, Victor; and I don't think you'd do that." The elder man was smiling as he spoke.

"I suppose if I try to get out of this trap, you'll knock me down and sit on me. But you know I can't go back on *you*. Oh, yes, Leroy is slick. That's what he's banking on, is it?"

"Why, you see, Victor," said Smith, " it ain't no use to git excited and throw open the throttle. If you do git back to Fairport to-morrow, by that time Harry'll have the strike all called off and the men will be back at work again, and it won't be so easy. No, Victor, Harry's got the brakes on and you got to quit, and you best quit easy. Ma's making them corn griddle-cakes you used to like so, and she's frying some sausages and potatoes and making coffee, and we got a good bed for you upstairs. And though it is a kinder queer way to meet again, and we wish you felt different about it, we're real glad to see you, Vi."

"If I must be in prison," said West, "I couldn't ask kinder jailers, that's sure!"

He smiled his radiant, winning smile; and it was a surprise to have Smith wince. Why? But he was chilled and hungry and there would be no harm in watching his chance to escape and meanwhile eating supper. He had no kinship with the Smiths, although he called them "Uncle" and "Aunt;" but when he came to Chicago, a lonely, ambitious orphan boy, he had boarded for five years with them. They were very kind to him. Years ago he had left them. At the time, his heart was warm, remembering a thousand little kindnesses, yes, and kindness not little; and he expected to keep up the old intimacy always. But they were shy people, and he was a busy, rising man. Somehow the wave had lifted him and washed them out of his sight. It had been years since he had seen them. Now, his keen eyes were all over the room questioning the furniture. That was the old photograph on the table that he used to show to Hughey.

No trace of Hughey, where was he? The colored photograph was little Maggie. But where was she? It would be awkward to ask and be told the child was dead. A sweet little creature she was, too, and so fond of him. He didn't like the looks of the room, either; everything neat as wax, to be sure, but the furniture wasn't the old furniture, it was cheap and new and awful little of it. The table spread for supper didn't have as pretty dishes as he remembered, and where were those "solid silver" spoons that had been Aunt Maggie's pride? He did hear that Smith had lost his engine in the '94 strike. Blacklisted, perhaps (and his heart swelled), "Papa Smith" as the boys called him, the most faithful man who ever rode an engine at death to save his passengers. He wished—but how could he keep track of folks that wouldn't try to look him up? Nevertheless, he began his inquiries at supper. "Uncle Phil," he said, "I tried to find you in '94, but you'd moved away."

"There!" cried the woman, impulsively, "I told you, pa!"

"So you did, ma," Smith admitted, "and I'm real glad you was right. Well, I knowed myself, Vi, if you knowed the fix we was in, you'd have come a running to help us, but *there!*"

"Why didn't you write me?"

Smith looked shamefacedly at his wife. "Why, fact is, I did write; asked if you happened to know of a job. But, fact is, I wasn't up to more than a postal card, then,"—he grinned awkwardly—"and I wrote it on that."

"I never got it," exclaimed West, promptly, but he changed color, remembering, abruptly, how he would let the typewriter sort over his mail; and how little attention was paid to postals. He hastened to say that he had once gone out to their house in Kenwood.

"Yes, I lost the house," said Smith; "pretty rough. I had it half paid for, and I had to sell it for two hundred and twenty dollars. You see the engineers wasn't out; but I went to hear 'Gene Debs one night, and he worked me up so I didn't see straight. Hadn't any grievance, but I couldn't bear to leave the boys, and they were calling me a scab, and that speech tumbled me off my base. I jumped off my engine when I found the soldiers was going on my train. More'n that, being plumb crazy, I went out with the crowd.

They were throwing rocks. *I* wasn't; but who was to know that? I looked up and I saw the old man himself, the president of the road, looking right at me. I s'pose they marked me down for a violent rioter, that minnit."

" And so they blacklisted you? "

" Well, you see there has been such a sight of men looking for jobs on railways, and such a awful few railroad jobs to give 'em that it was no more than nature for the railroads to stand by the men who'd stood by them, and give the other fellers who had made 'em such a lot of trouble the marble heart. And I got it. I'd an awful hard time. Once or twice I got a engine, sorter scrub engine, of course; but in a little while I'd be laid off. God knows whether 'twas the blacklist or they really didn't have the work, like they said. I had to go, anyway. We'd a hard time, Vi, a awful hard time. Ma, she went out as scrub-woman, she did, when we was at the worst—after little Maggie died. She caught cold one day and had a bad cough, and it got worse and—that's how. I ain't been the same man since, I guess. You remember how Maggie and me—I guess there never was a parent set more by a child; and there never was a child was better or brighter—and always laughing, don't you remember, Vi? fall down and hurt herself and scramble up on her little fat legs and lift up her little face with her lip a quivering, but laughing. 'Pa and Maggie don't cry!' says she—because I said that to her after I got burned in the accident, you know; she was pitying me so. And she made it her own word, ever afterward."

"I hope—I wish I could have done something—Uncle Phil, this is awful!"

"She had every comfort, Victor," said Mrs. Smith.

"Yes, she did," said Smith, "'twas then I sold the house."

"And Hughey? Couldn't he help you?"

Mrs. Smith said something about cakes, and rose hastily, in spite of West's protest that he didn't wish any more cakes.

"I guess you ain't heard about Hughey, Victor"—sinking his voice—"don't speak about it before ma. You—you're about the only one of our friends I'd be willing to have know it, but I guess you know the sorter boy Hughey was, and you won't be hard on him; he jest went crazy, Hughey did—in that strike. He threw up his job's fireman; and after the strike was over he got to running with a awful bad lot that cursed all the rich folks and said that property was robbery, and poor Hughey, he was always that tender-hearted you know, always from a child; and he fairly went wild. He heard about a job in Fairport, at Cochrane's, fireman to the stationary engineer. He didn't git much wages and his crazy friends was always at him. Well—they'd a safe, of course. There was two men, they got at Hughey. They got round him." The father looked appealingly at West. " You know how easy it was to git round Hughey. And he didn't think it was wrong. That's how it was. They caught them. Hughey only's got a year. Ma's been to see him. She says he feels a good deal changed. Harry Leroy, he's been awful good to him. He was a good friend of his at the trial, too. Telling about how faithful Hughey was at his work. Harry's been awful good to Hughey. It might be worse, don't you think, Vi? Cochrane says he'll take him back and give him another show. And Harry's talking to him 'bout them notions of his. I—would it be too much trouble for you when you're in Fairport to go see him, Vi? He thinks a lot of you. He used to git all your speeches when they'd come out in the papers."

"I'll be glad to go," said West. He spoke the truth; any kindness to the Smiths would be a relief to his conscience. "But, see here, yourself?" West asked, "isn't there any way I can help *you?*"

Smith's brow cleared; he smiled like the old "Papa Smith" West used to know.

"That's jest like you. Ma! Victor's got his hand in his pocket"—which was true—"he wants to give us some of his mun."

"Not on your life, Vi," called Mrs. Smith, heartily. She pattered in, her hands full. Her eyes were red, but she was smiling. "You're jest the same Vi, if you have got famous. You keep your money; we don't need it, pa's got a good job—Pa, you tell Vi how you got your job!"

It was a relief to have Smith plunge into the new subject with a glance at his wife and a sputtering laugh. "Why, it was this way, Victor. I'd been tramping for most two years when I run into a job here. Got a stationary engine. Dirt train. She was the worst old terror I ever struck, running loose all the time, and kicking up sech a noise you'd think she'd

"THEY CAUGHT THEM. HUGHEY ONLY'S GOT A YEAR."

bust, next minnit. But I was awful glad to git her. And I did my darndest to please and hold my job. Hung on all spring, all summer. Feeling kinder easy when, one day, who should I see in front of me but the old man. Him! The pipe tumbled out of my mouth and me on all fours after it, to pick up the pieces. I felt like I was all crumpled up. He never said a word to me. No more I never said a word to him. Picked up the pieces of that pipe and he was gone off. First I thought I wouldn't tell ma; then, I thought I wouldn't want her keeping things from me; and I remembered we'd been through a good deal together; and, fact is, I *had* to tell her. And she advised me right straight to tell the old man the whole story, 'bout little Maggie and all. But I couldn't bring myself to that. I went back next day, in an awful sweat, figuring on brassing it out as John Smith. And I guess you could have wrung me out like a wet rag when I seen the old man bearing down on me. He's a little, fleshy man, and wears a brown overcoat that never's buttoned; and before the strike I used to think he was a real pleasant gentleman, and often had a word with him. He used to be a poor boy himself, you know. But, that day, when I seen him steering for me, and thought of Maggie at home and all the misery I'd seen, I was equal to murdering him, if we'd been off by ourselves. He was on me before I had got my story clear in my mind. 'What's the matter with that engine, Phil?' says he.

"'Nothing but age,' says I—then it come to me, I'd answered to my name. You see a man gits so infernally used to his own name it's hard to drop it. 'My name ain't Phil,' says I, 'it's John William, they most generally call me John, here'—yes, they did, too, and lots of trouble I had remembering, and plenty of times I didn't remember and wouldn't answer quick. But, there, I stood scowling at him and wondering whether I wouldn't break his head if he gave me the bounce and, 'My name's John William Smith,' says I. 'You used to be an honest man, Phil,' says he, 'when I knew you. I was so sure of you in the strike I told Kane to have an engine ready for you, I knew *you* wouldn't be scared.' Then, somehow, I remembered what ma said and it didn't seem so hard to do it; and it all come out. I told him the whole story, black list and all; and I stuck my eyes on the buttons in his vest—his overcoat was a flying, way it always had, no matter what the weather—and I couldn't see how he was taking it; but what I did see was three men come bustling up to him. And I stopped short and looked up at him; the men were right in hearing. What do you think he said? He said, 'That's all right, Phil!' It turned me so queer I most couldn't keep on my feet; and I couldn't tell either what he meant to do; but that night I found out, for the agent he come out and says he, 'You're always scouring up that old tub, Smith, but I guess I'd let the new man do that, to-night.' 'What in h—— do you mean?' says I, but I guessed I knew, else I wouldn't have spoke so rough; and I guess he did, too, for he laughed out, 'You lost your job, Smith; but you've got a better, you're to take out No. 253 on the freight in future; and you better be slinging your oil-can over there where it is waiting!' You bet I didn't mind them laughing at me, then. And yet, when I seen the president, that very next morning, me leaning out of my cab and feeling like—well, I can't tell you how I felt feeling an engine under me that could *go!*—will you believe I jest couldn't say nothing, couldn't do nothing but

swaller and swaller and look like a fool.
' That's all right, Phil,' says he, again, and off
before I could git my tongue loose."

West was not as ready as usual with a reply; but he said that he was heartily glad
Phil had his job back again. "I'm to have a
passenger next month," said Phil, "I've got
all my dues paid up. I'm square with the
union. But, I guess you can see why I ain't
stuck on strikes. And maybe a little why I'm
helping Harry."

"I see," said West. He made an excuse to
go up to his own room for a few moments
while Mrs. Smith washed the dishes. He stood
in the centre of the bare little room and
thought hard. He was accustomed to regard
himself as an honest man, a soldier of humanity, to be frank, as a fine fellow—only we
never coarsely tell ourselves that we are fine
fellows, we simply feel it, as we feel cold or
warm or hungry. West had felt the delicate
intoxication of satisfied vanity; but he had
never imagined the glow and the elation to
come from vanity; he credited it all to an approving conscience. Now, he looked at a
strike from Harry Leroy's point of view.
Poor Hughey! what a tender-hearted little

"BUT, THERE, I STOOD SCOWLING AT HIM AND WONDERING WHETHER I WOULDN'T BREAK HIS HEAD."

chap he was in those days, with a funny little face that would tie itself up in knots of anguish over West's tales of kidnapped children. And how Hughey and Mrs. Smith used to cheer him, that first year when he was admitted to the United Brotherhood of Carpenters, No. 8, by listening breathlessly to all his speeches and weeping all through the speech he made for Hiram Dixon's funeral. It was a little more than he had bargained to pay for his pathos, however, to have Mrs. Smith give up the treat she had planned and spend all the cyclorama money for flowers "for that poor motherless lad you were telling us about, Vi." Dixon was really only a subject for oratory to Victor; but he suppressed his feelings and wove Mrs. Smith's and Hughey's self-denial into his speech; later, with gratifying effect. His heart softened, remembering how the two, mother and son, always came any distance to hear him speak. Often he would see the little woman and the boy sitting as near as they could get; their faces glowing at every sentence. He could see the proud glances they exchanged! And how happy they seemed on those few nights—confound it! why were they not more?—when

Victor would make part of the toilsome car journey back with them!

Once, Mrs. Smith had looked troubled; she even adventured a timid criticism at the end of the lecture. "Ain't you a little too hard on the plutograts, Vi? Some of them are good men, and I've known of their doing kind things right here in Chicago. You know Hughey takes everything you say for gospel." He wasn't to blame for Hughey. No, he wouldn't take that load on his soul; the other men, the cursed railroad sharks—he laughed uneasily—or the cursed fools who ran men into a hopeless strike. And yet he wished that he had kept an eye on the Smiths. But he was so infernally busy, studying and working, burning the candle at both ends; and they never pushed themselves. Why didn't they push themselves a little? they had no right to expect him to do all the seeking out, why didn't they hunt him up in their distresses? But he stopped in the middle of a phrase; for he remembered when the Smiths did hunt him up; when he was hurt by the car and lay for a month at the hospital. Never a visiting day passed that one of them did not come, always with some little offering. Little Maggie worked him a pin-cushion and Hughey drew on his hoard at the savings bank to buy a bottle of port wine, and Smith had spent a whole afternoon, taking him to drive. West sank down in a chair and groaned. No, curse it, there was no use excusing himself; Leroy had been a better friend to these trusting, loyal souls than he. For one sickening moment, Leroy seemed to have the right of it in other ways. Then, his confidence in himself righted; but it had changed places in that searing light. He pushed the vision out of his mind, yet he never again could be so lightly sure of his own judgment. And he knew it. With a long, long sigh, he rose. He called to Smith; and when the latter answered him, he said, speaking a trifle more rapidly than his wont: "Say, Uncle Phil, your friend Leroy has more sense on his side than I thought; will you get me off in time to catch the train for Fairport, if I'll give you my parole not to oppose Leroy, but let them settle the strike their own way?"

Smith did not hesitate. "Why, that's what Harry told me to do, keep you here till you'd give your word not to fight him. He said he knowed you was white. He didn't expect you'd come round 'fore morning; but I don't see as it makes any difference. I'll let you out; and—say, if you'll promise not to stop Harry, you can take the freight-train to Fairport. I'll put you 'board."

"And we'll talk about Hughey on the way," resolved West.

. . . .

The rougher shook his head, while he jammed the tobacco into his pipe with his thumb. "Queerest thing I ever did see. And West was as smooth as you'd want. How'd Harry fix him?"

Thompson, to whom he spoke, wagged his head first at him, next at the carpenter. "I don't know any mor'n you do. Harry asked me to drive the hack. And I drove it. He got in like a lamb. They may have mixed a bit inside; but he got out like a lamb, when we got there. Then I had orders to drive off and get to Fairport in time for the meeting. I did it, too."

"All I know," said the carpenter, rubbing his chin, "is that Bob and I were to watch at the house and not let him git out; and when Smith gave the word, *we* were to cut for Fairport. He didn't do a thing. And Smith gave

us the word; and we took the cars for the depot and came on to Fairport for the meeting; and everything went like it had been greased."

"That's right," said the steel man, lighting his pipe and puffing thoughtfully. "And all I know, it 'twas West I reckoned would get there; and he was so much smarter than Harry; and yet Henry's got onto it with both feet."

"Maybe another time, you won't be blaming Harry so much for not being fiery," Thompson observed, a second later—the interval having been filled with smoke and meditation—" and you won't sock at him that he's so blamed law and orderly!"

"We won't," said the rougher, "and what's more, if Harry says Law and Order, Law and Order it's going to be, if we have to bust all the other fellers' heads!"

JOHNNY'S JOB

JOHNNY'S JOB

THE day was so warm that the men at the steel-works were all mopping their brows with the back of their hands. Nevertheless the furnaces were flaming and the great red and black iron sheds were penetrated with the incessant pounding roar of the rolls.

Johnny Burke, the new heater's-helper, cast a keen glance out of his long-lashed Irish gray eyes at Larsen, the heater. The tall Swede's face was flushed and strange of expression; he flung his tools noisily into the bosh. Both the drag-down and the charger glanced askance at him, exchanging opinions in pantomime; but Johnny did not speak to either of them, he walked over to the roller. That great man was tapping the rolls with his tongs, whistling softly.

"Say," said Johnny in his ear, "something's the matter with Larsen, he ain't been round to reverse the furnace for half an hour.

I reversed it, myself, a little while ago, I didn't like to before; but the bridge was 'most awash—all melting!"

The roller nodded. "I told the rougher the next piece of hard iron he got from him to send it back; he would before only he's a friend of Knute's. Well, so'm I a friend of Knute's; but we can't have the turn spoiled with cracked iron."

"Looks like he had a jag on him," said Johnny, in a dispassionate way.

"That's it," the roller returned gloomily, "he's had some sort of trouble with his wife. Jealous *I* guess; and he was drinking yesterday. Never knew him to drink before. But these sober fellers when they get to drinking, go all to pieces. It's an awful pity. Knute's a pretty good feller. Say, do you think you can kinder watch the furnace? Go right ahead, he won't notice!"

"I guess so," said Johnny; but his heart swelled within him. "I had a heater's job last."

"How'd you lose it?"

"Strike. We lost it; and they didn't take on all the men. There was a lot of married men wanted to get back, bad; they didn't want to move. And I was single and footloose—so I skipped. Well, maybe "—flushing with his effort to be candid—" maybe they wouldn't have took me on if I'd asked. I didn't ask."

"I guess you're white," said the roller; "well, keep your eye on things!"

He gazed after Johnny's curly black head and handsome profile with a new interest, but far from suspecting that he had heard the disappointment of Johnny's life. To be sure Johnny had said nothing of the girl.

Johnny was a new man, taken on a week ago, on Leroy's recommendation. Leroy was an old friend of Knute Larsen's. Knute was popular in the works, not only in his own little realm, the eight-inch mill, where the heater has almost equal powers with the roller, but in the other mills and in the office. To the office there was one exception, the assistant superintendent. He was a young man who rated his own knowledge high. During the superintendent's absence he was in charge; and he had already had a dispute with Knute about the "scrap." The "scrap" was of his own adventurous buying; and, naturally, when the turns were disappointing he blamed the heaters, blamed the rollers, and blamed Knute Larsen more than all.

Knute, however, only blamed the "scrap;" he did not pass his superior's bad temper on to Johnny; and Johnny was grateful.

He respected Larsen, not only because he was a remarkably good heater, who always sent out "nice soft iron," but because he was tall—Johnny, himself, being very short. Knute had soft blue eyes and a yellow beard. He was taciturn but cheerful in his silent way; and liked to listen to other men's jokes, smiling with his eyes. The last man one would think, to jeopard his high wages by drinking. "A married man, too," thought Johnny severely, "if I ever get married"—he flushed and his eyes sparkled; and he stood for a moment absently gazing at nothing, while his whole life seemed to drift before him.

First he saw himself a little straightening boy, barely nine, dizzy with the glory of working in an iron-mill and having wages of his own to bring home to his mother, every fortnight. His father was dead. He had three sisters, all younger than he; he was the man of the family, his mother always called him "Mother's man." His poor mother! even after all those years the lump climbed into Johnny's throat as he remembered how the three little sisters had all died in one dreadful week of diphtheria, and how he stood alone by his mother, beside the last and smallest little grave. Somehow the shade of little Rosy "who was so cute" was most vivid to him of all; and his mother's grief for her baby was heartbreaking. "But I've got you, son," she sobbed, "mother's little man—O Johnny, be *careful!*"

I fear Johnny was hardly careful in the way that she meant; he had the name of "the recklessest little devil in the works;" and his mother's hair would have turned gray could she have viewed him cheerily dodging the wriggling, glowing red serpents that dove at him from the finishing rolls. But he was careful of his mother; he learned to put a stout front on his hardships, to keep his kicks and cuffs to himself and hide his burns and get up in the black winter mornings without calling, although his muscles had not rested from last night's ache; and he would make faces for the pain, while he dressed. He thought of none of those things now; his lips were working and he brushed the wet out of his eyes because he remembered how happy his mother was when he was made strand boy, happier than she had been since the little girls died. She laughed, she laughed out loud! "Think of you only thirteen and earning most as much as your ma! Oh, if your pa could see you this day! If he could know how you've been mother's man"—and then she kissed him and sorely scared him by crying bitterly. Was it, as she said, for the joy and for remembering how proud his father had always been of his only son, or was it because she knew she had the sickness on her? "I'm glad I got the raise that week," muttered Johnny, his eyes dimming. Next week, he had no mother to be glad for him. He went to live with his aunt. She was sorry for the lad, who made no complaints and only cried at night for his mother, but she had married a widower with six small children, each one, she was accustomed to say, bad in a different way from the others, so she had scant leisure for "mothering" Johnny. At fifteen Johnny felt himself a man; and not a youngster in the works got so many cuffs and oaths from the roughers whose tongs he was using the minute their backs were turned. Plenty of kindness the roughers gave him, between deserved reproofs for meddling; and he picked up ambition and rude notions of honor and a reverence for the Amalgamated Association. The Lodge of the Association and the Lodge of the Knights of Pythias gave Johnny most of his education, both moral and intellectual. Never did either association or order have a catechumen who listened more eagerly to teachings of the fraternal duties of brothers in the lodge.

"It's the most wonderful thing in the world," mused Johnny often, during the first years of his membership. "Well, I guess there's one thing that beats 'em all," he thought to-day, "beats even the knights." And Johnny sighed. For that one thing was love. When Johnny was twenty-three, he fell in love. It was soon after he got his job as heater; and a light heart is easy to move. She was a clerk in a dry-goods shop; our English cousins would call it a haberdasher's. She boarded at Mrs. Heller's, only two blocks away from Johnny's aunt's house, a clean, quiet place, very respectable and not expensive. Johnny still boarded with his aunt. He could have found a pleasanter place for his money; and he didn't enjoy the nightly com-

panionship of his youngest cousin, known in
the family circle as "Kicker;" but no one
else would sleep with the child, and his aunt
needed the board money; hence Johnny
stayed and paid it, scrupulously in advance.
He furnished his bare little room, making it
so comfortable that his aunt always gave it to
her mother-in-law when she visited them,
while Johnny camped elsewhere—with Kicker.
The girl, Miss Dora Glenn (Johnny knew
her name before he knew her), rode a bicycle.
Johnny also rode a bicycle; and almost daily,
returning from his work, he met Miss Glenn
returning from hers. He admired her riding;
then he admired her. One day, his heart
curdled beholding a desperate "object-
struck" beginner, a man of herculean frame,
charge down on a baby carriage, and Miss
Glenn pedal swiftly in between the doomed in-
fant and the human catapult. Johnny scorching down to her, arrived in time to see the
collision and to hear the crash. She was not
hurt—the man had toppled over at a touch;
one can scarcely say that he lost his balance,
he having so little balance to lose—but her
wheel was broken. Johnny mended it; after
he had given the unhappy beginner his opin-

JOHNNY MENDED IT.

ion of a man that couldn't steer, coming out on the street. "You best *walk* home," says Johnny sternly; "and be thankful you ain't a murderer; you ain't safe on a wheel!"

The giant limped meekly away, pushing his unharmed wheel; while Johnny addressed himself to repairs, assisted by Miss Glenn. She had taken off her gloves. Once her hand touched his. It was a very white hand and felt cool and lovely smooth; and somehow, although it was so different, Johnny's memory flashed back to the touch of his mother's hand on his cheek. "Ma'd like her," he thought. "Oh, I wish I could tell ma about her."

He noticed that she did not talk like the Pennsylvania girls; and long afterward, the rich, leisurely cadences of her voice lived on his ear. He always thought of her with a reflection of the tingling throb his heart gave him, as she flew past, straight into the path of that mountain of a man.

"Knew he'd bowl her over, but bound to save the baby!" thought Johnny enthusiastically. "Oh, ain't she got sand! And she's a perfect lady, too."

After this incident, whenever they met she

smiled and Johnny took off his cap. The second week he ventured to observe the road was bad for wheeling, or it was a warm day, merely in passing. He thought about her a great deal; and he thought more about his mother and his father than he had in a long time. He consulted a carpenter of his acquaintance in regard to the price of houses. At the lodge of the association, during the social half hour after the business session, he made one of the most vigorous speeches ever there made, on the subject of steel men wasting their wages in riotous good times. As Johnny, while never known to be visibly under the influence of that which biteth like a serpent and stingeth like an adder, had prided himself on the hardness of his head rather than on keeping out of temptation, and, indeed, had been nicknamed "the tank" by less capable and envious drinkers, this austerity drew much talk. Johnny, himself, felt that he had burned his festive bridges behind him.

The following week he had two photographs taken (in his uniform as a Knight of Pythias, his hand on his sword hilt). Saturday night he put the best two of the dozen in his pocket and after an hour of scrubbing and dressing, took his way to the Hellers.

It was a June night; and Miss Glenn might be sitting out on the piazza with the family. So in truth it fell out. Miss Glenn was rocking beside Mrs. Heller.

They both rose to greet him. He had never seen her except on her wheel or beside it. Her trailing shimmering black skirt made her look very tall; and there was a dainty air about her pink shirt-waist and snowy lawn tie. "She's an elegant appearing lady!" thought Johnny, making his best bow to the accompaniment of Mrs. Heller's introduction.

"So you ain't married yet?" says Mrs. Heller, by way of setting everyone at ease.

"No, ma'am; but I'm thinking of it," says Johnny, forcing his eyes up to Miss Glenn's face and turning scarlet. It seemed to him that he had almost made her an offer of his hand. He cleared his husky voice and plunged ahead. "I'm getting six and seven dollars a day; and I hope to make more when I get used to heating. I've got a hundred and twenty-two dollars in the bank. I don't think a man has got any right to marry unless he can give his wife a house of their own."

If his voice would not roll up like a ball in his throat he could say more, a great deal more; but how could he talk when he had to keep swallowing? He essayed a smile—at Mrs. Heller; and he felt the drops rolling down his neck and wilting his beautiful white collar.

"That's awful good wages," said Mrs. Heller cordially.

"I should *say!*" Miss Glenn agreed. Again to-day he felt the glow of her bright dark eyes on him; and his heart bounded.

"You must be high up, Johnny," said Mrs. Heller; "rougher or heater—you'd never get that much, finishing."

"Sure," said Johnny modestly, "I'm heater for the twelve-inch——"

"My! but you're young to be a heater, Johnny! Wasn't you scared first day you went on? You know Heller was a heater, and he told me he was dreadful scared the first week lest he'd burn the breast out of the furnace or some sech awful thing."

"Well, I was too," admitted Johnny. "I guess I ain't all over being scared, yet; you see there are so many bad things you can do, to the furnace or the iron."

"That's so," the heater's widow assented,

shaking her head; " you're jest like your pa, Johnny, so conscientious."

Johnny, in an access of gratitude, pulled out the photographs and asked her if she could give them house-room. He remembered with a thrill how Miss Glenn's graceful brown head looked, bent over the pictures. He remembered how he lost his constraint and waxed fluent explaining the objects of the Knights of Pythias. But he could not muster daring enough to ask her to accept one of the pictures. Instead out of his grateful heart, he asked Mrs. Heller, her daughter, and her little son (too young to be left at home) and Miss Glenn to go driving Sunday afternoon; and he took them in a surrey with two handsome horses that the clerk of the livery stable told him were never allowed to go without a stable driver; but he said that for a dollar extra he, Johnny, being known to be a careful man, should be given the fiery steeds. Johnny did not find them fiery; but he had the pleasure of passing over the clerk's cautions to Mrs. Heller; and she sat on the back seat with her children, clasping them in her arms and calling " whoa! " loudly every time one of the horses lashed a fly; and Miss Dora was on the front seat with him; and the gates of paradise swung open.

But the days went by without his adventuring any further confusion. Twice he rode in the park with her, once on Saturday evening, once on Sunday afternoon. He told her of his parents, of his hopes, of his ambitions, he told her of everything but his love; and that was so timid, so worshipful that he could not bring himself to speech. She told him that she was an orphan with one sister who was married and always begging her to try for employment in the town where she lived. "Sometimes I think I will," she said. "I was born West and I love it there; I get homesick for the Mississippi River. I hate the big cities—like this. I love a town where there are trees on the streets and all the folks have yards to their houses. And I *love* to see the river."

"Yes, a river's a great thing," said Johnny. "I don't know when I learned to swim, I was so little. Once we lived right on the river and my mother was so 'fraid I'd get drownded. But she wasn't after she saw me swim."

"Mrs. Heller says you saved a little boy from drowning, once."

"'Shaw, that was nothing, the kid fell in the

cistern and all I had to do was to tread water."
Johnny was tempted to tell of the man that he
had saved in the river; but he thought that
would look like bragging and held his peace.

She was riding, slowly, her eyes on the grass-
plots that swam before them as they passed.
Her brown hair took sunnier glints in the twi-
light glow, the delicate oval of her cheek was
flushed. She was pretty, as thousands of
American girls are pretty, but in that light,
with the gentle thought in her eyes, she looked
an angel to her lover. He caught his breath.
"If I get married, my wife shall live where
she pleases if I can only get good work," said
he, frowning and grasping the handle-bar with
a grip of steel.

He did not see her face or he would have
seen that she grew red; but she laughed and
exclaimed, "Oh, what a beautiful road to
scorch!"

Johnny could not understand whether she
wanted to put him off; but he was too shy to
persist. He bent over his handle-bar.

The next day the long-threatening strike began. Johnny had no job; no right, he
thought, to speak. "I'll wait until we win
and I'm back," he said. And they did not

win. That was a hard month to Johnny, a hard decision to make, to relinquish his fair hopes and go on the road for a job. But, swearing at his luck, Johnny chose a heavy heart instead of a loaded conscience; and went dismally to Mrs. Heller to tell them that he must go. "My sakes alive!" cried Mrs. Heller, waving her pudgy hands in the air, "didn't you know it? Miss Glenn's *gone*. Her sister's been writing and writing; and she decided yesterday she'd go. She left her good-by for you; and hoped if you was ever in Fairport, Ia., you'd come to see her."

Johnny's cheeks were a kind of blue white. His teeth came together with a click. His nostrils widened. Mrs. Heller turned away from his miserable eyes.

"I—I give her one of your photographs afore she went, Johnny," said she; "you don't mind."

Johnny laughed. "I guess I don't. I guess you're an awful good friend of mine. Good-by, Mrs. Heller, a friend of mine knows a Mr. Leroy in Fairport. He's president of the Labor Council; and I'll get a letter to him. There's a new steel works in Fairport or just 'cross the river. I'm going to try for a

" MISS GLENN'S GONE."

job there. What—what's Miss Dora's address?"

But Miss Dora had left no address. " Maybe's a little town; and I don't need it," said Johnny stoutly. He took the night train for the West, leaving consolation gifts for his weeping aunt and the cousins, and carrying away a very scanty remainder of his savings. " Oh, I'll get along," he said to the boys at the train; and he would not borrow and went away smiling; and nobody saw the puckered face bent over the back of the car-seat as the flaming chimneys fell behind. " Think of them boys, who are all stone-broke and just got their jobs back, wanting to lend *me* money," he gurgled to the roar of the train. " I'll never find no such friends anywhere else!"

He was desperately lonely the first week in Fairport. He would have been more lonely but for Harry Leroy, who asked him once to supper at his own house and gave him a good word with Knute Larsen and the superintendent of the Edgewater Steel Works, and lent him papers to read.

He walked the streets and rode on the street-railways and bought papers of pins or thread or needles or a cake of soap in every dry-goods shop in the city of Fairport; but not once did he see the face that haunted his heart.

Not once until this morning; and because of this morning, because of an eyeblink of a face at a car-window whirling by—just as he turned to go his way to the works—he stood now viewing the panorama of his life, and sure that for this all had been worth the living.

He roused himself to attend to the drafts of the furnace. Knute was lurching about in a heavy-gaited way smiling feebly did anyone speak to him; and making futile attempts to focus his glassy eyeballs on the speaker.

"You go to the window and get a breath of air," said Johnny. "I'll talk to the boss."

"Where's Larsen?" said the assistant superintendent.

"He's 'most sick to-day; it's so hot."

"It's infernal weather," grumbled the young man; but he looked after Knute's swaying back in a way that Johnny did not like.

A few minutes later Johnny, having gone to the window himself for a gasp of relief from the dead heat of the mill, heard the assistant and the time-keeper talking. They were in the roadway below and did not see him.

"I guess there is," the time-keeper was saying in answer to some question. "I noticed he was wrong when I was in there, taking time; he couldn't hardly answer me; but it may be the heat."

"Doesn't look like it," said the assistant; "if he is drunk, he'll go, that's all. It's too cursed risky! Johnny Burke used to be a heater and he can take the place. I'm not going to have a mess at the eight-inch to report to the old man, to-morrow." They passed on; and Johnny went back to the furnace thinking, "I'll give Knute a hint; he ain't showing good sense."

But there was Knute, prone on the sand-heap beside the furnace, in the scorching heat, his purple face full in the glow. Johnny did not look at his face. He looked, his eyes hardening, at the photograph slipping out of the drunken hand. It was a woman's face; and the face was Dora Glenn's. Johnny set his teeth and strode to the window. There was a throbbing in the back of his head; he couldn't breathe.

"Trouble with his wife!" And Dora was

his wife. They hadn't been married a month; yet he was quarrelling with her and getting drunk. He felt no anger against the girl. "She didn't promise me nothing," he groaned, "she ain't to blame for me being a fool.—Oh God! I didn't have a *look* from her that I got the right to remember against her." It was a forlorn comfort that she wasn't to blame. She wasn't to blame with that brute, either. He knew that. A sickening rage at the man who could treat her so turned him dizzy. "I'll not lift a hand for him"—that was his first conscious thought—"I won't scab any man's job; but I am not going to try to save his for him, he can take his chances by——!"

Out of the corner of his eye he had a vision of the young boss at the straightening beds. "I ain't going to look round," said Johnny, doggedly. Therefore he stared out of the window in time to see Harry Leroy on his way to the office with a message about the Cochrane Company's steel. Leroy sent him a friendly smile and a hail; "Don't forget you take supper with me, Saturday. We'll have chicken!"

Johnny's head sank. He waited a second longer. "Oh Lord, I *got* to do it," he groaned. "I couldn't look him in the face if I didn't. Knute's a brother knight, too!"

With that he rushed off to Knute. The assistant superintendent was walking toward him from the other direction. But Johnny reached the insensible man first, had the whiskey flask out and was bathing the purple face, at the same instant calling loudly on Bill the drag-down and George the charger.

"Get him to the faucet, get some ice water!" roared Johnny above the din; "he's prostrated by the heat! Tell the boss, some of you boys!"

"Whiskey sunstroke I guess," said the superintendent, sniffing.

"I was bathing him with it," Johnny explained promptly; "he was hot and dry's a board!"

"That's it," agreed the roller, bustling up, "he complained of his head to me, this morning."

"And he said he couldn't sweat a mite and he felt all burning up!" chimed in George; while Bill proffered testimony in the same strain. The united stress of opinion was too much for the assistant superintendent's nerve; after all, it might be sunstroke, anyhow the men would swear that it was; and there was the old man to consider; he watched them drenching Knute with ice-water; and all he said was, "He's coming round all right. He better go home," and so walked away.

But Knute had his own mind about going home. He opened his eyes, into which the light was creeping, and stared at Johnny. "Did I lose my job?" said he.

"No; you're all right," said Johnny.

"You boys kept it for me? It vas 'bout my vife. See's good vomans, but see's gone back on me. See? I guess I kill myself."

"Oh, rats!" said Johnny. "Here, get up; the boss thinks it sunstroke and you can go home."

"No, I don't go home," said Knute, sitting up, "the old mans, fore he vent, said to try to git sixty t'ousand of half-inch round—I git it, dis turn. Dot's vy I drink—to make me strong, 'cause my head is wrong dis hot wedder."

Despite the roller's protestations he staggered to his feet. "Yonny vill help me," he said, "I git along."

As for Johnny, he laid every nerve to work to guard Larsen, and to make his estimate of

"I WAS BATHING HIM WITH IT," JOHNNY EXPLAINED, PROMPTLY.

the turn good. He would not think; he would not feel; he had the billets to watch and the furnace. Sixty thousand was a big turn. But when the weight was posted on the board, Bill and George came to slap him on the back as well as Larsen; and Larsen's eyes brightened. He was quite sober, now. " I'm mooch obliged to you boys," he said, " dot's a good turn. Yonny is a good heater. Good-by."

He shook hands with the roller and the finisher, with the roughers and his own helpers. Then, he took out his knife and handed it to one of the straightening boys, saying, " You got dat knife, Hughey, I gif him to you."

Hughey grinned; but the men exchanged uneasy glances and talked to each other, as Knute walked off to his locker for his coat. They would have drafted Johnny into the conversation, but he had slipped outside. " It's none of my business if he does try to kill himself, best thing for her, I guess." In this fashion he muttered to himself, nevertheless not mending his pace, going more slowly, in fact, with each word. " Supposing he is a brother knight—it's none of my business." He stood still. " The way those Pittsburg knights stood by me ain't got nothing to do

with it!" He turned on his heel. "D——
it!" He walked back to the works.

Little groups of the men were all along the
road, and in the second group he saw George
the charger lending a sympathetic arm to
Knute, Bill and the roller walking on the other
side. The roller's brow cleared at sight of
Johnny; he lagged behind for a moment's
confidence. "We're going to put Knute on
the car that goes to his house; I guess he'll be
all right, then, don't you?"

"I guess you and I best get on the car with
him, on the sly. Maybe he didn't mean nothing by his talk, but Swedes kill themselves awful easy."

"That's right," sighed the roller. "Well,
my wife is sure there's been an accident if I'm
ten minutes behind time, but I'll go with you;
we'll let Georgy and Bill go home."

George and Bill accordingly put Knute on
the car, after Johnny and the roller had
nodded good-by, and Knute had insisted on
shaking hands over again, not saying anything
except, "I vas much obliged," to each. There
was no difficulty in getting a rear position on
the strap; and Knute, in front, did not suspect
his two comrades' presence. He sat with his

eyes on the brick pavements and the maple trees, and the houses half-hidden by the foliage. "It's singular," mused the roller, with the artless confidence of the average street-car traveller that his remarks will reach no other ear than that into which they are poured, "it's singular the trouble women make the most sensible men. Now till just lately, since he's been married, I'd have bet money on Knute's sense. But he's crazy over this girl. She *is* pretty; but she's kinder giddy, I guess, too, nothing wrong, just thoughtless. I saw her once out riding on her wheel and a floor-walker down at Kingman's was riding with her, a pretty little feller all dressed up in plaid stockings. Now Knute's not pretty. I guess he didn't like it. He fairly worshipped her, though. You ought to see the house he bought! He gave her a gold watch and chain —say, what's he doing now? Can you see?"

Johnny reported; "He's writing on a leaf of his memorandum-book. He's torn it out and folded it up; and now, he's putting it into an envelope that's addressed already—in ink."

"That don't look right a little bit."

Johnny shook his head. It was queer, but

a reluctant compassion was wrestling with the jealous hatred that clawed at his heart. Knute loved her, too. *He* had meant to give her a gold watch and chain for a wedding gift; but Knute had given it to her, instead. "He's getting up!" said the roller.

"S'posing he sees us, coming out!" said Johnny. But Larsen left the car by the other door. They followed him to the street, and kept him in sight from a safe distance. He went into the post-office, came out directly, walked a short block and signalled a bridge car. The bridge cars cross the Mississippi to Fairport.

"My wife will have a fit," moaned the roller, "but we've got to see this thing through. Ketch on, Johnny, and don't let him see you!"

They stood on the rear platform; and, as before, Larsen was sitting well in front, where they could only see the back of his head. He sat motionless, his gaze on the water, which was now kindling myriad opalescent hues under the golden torch in the west. A procession of wagons, carriages, phaetons, and last of all, one smart victoria with jingling chains on the horses' harness and a beautiful, dark-haired woman sitting behind the coachman (who plainly suffered in his livery) drifted past them on the opposite roadway. "She looks a little like Knute's wife," said the roller; "did you see Knute's shoulders jump? Say, I'm getting nervous."

"So am I," said Johnny; "but we're most across—he's up!"

He was up, reaching for the cord, stopping the car. He turned and passed them. "He'll wonder what we're doing here," the roller whispered, leaning on Johnny's nimbler wit. "What had we better say? You answer!"

But Knute's eyes turned, once, full on them, did not waver nor lighten; he went by with his strained, unseeing gaze; and nothing in the grisly chase had given them the chill of this blind passage. Their eyes met. "By ——, he means to do it," the roller said, under his breath; and Johnny nodded, rising. They were on the bridge floor, not a minute behind the Swede; but he was already standing at the further side of the railing.

"Larsen, *stop!*" shouted Johnny, vaulting over after him.

He never looked back; he flung his arms above his head and sprang. At the very instant of motion Johnny's hands grabbed his flannel shirt; but the stuff parted, and Johnny was reeling with the splash in his ears. The roller clutched him to save him from a fall. "Get a boat!" cried Johnny. "*I* can hold him—le' go!"

He had sprung after Knute, but in very different shape, circling like an arrow, his hands, like the arrow-head, protecting his body as he dived. How lucky his coat was on his arm instead of on his shoulders! How lucky he had untied his shoes in the cars on the suspicion of this very need; they were kicked off in a second! Where was the fellow's head? *There!* Look at him thrashing with his long arms! How his eyes bulged!

"Keep still! I'll save you!" yelled Johnny; and all the while his arms went like oars, and each magnificent kick of his steel-like legs was hurling him through the water.

He came up behind Knute; but even as his hand was outstretched the head sank. He dived for it, and it rose to the surface, dripping, the hair flat on the forehead, the face no longer a man's, only a mask of fear, with bared teeth, and painted eyeballs.

"Now you're all right!" called Johnny,

cheerfully. " I got you. Quit kicking, or I'll duck you! "

It is said that suicides are easy to save, having used up all their will-power in the last desperate act. Knute hardly struggled, for which one may give the reason cited, or take Johnny's praise for fact. " You're acting bully! " cried Johnny. " You know you don't want to drown *me*, too! "

He could hear voices and the frantic rattle and splash of oars. The danger went to his Irish blood like whiskey. " I'm all right," he sang out; " you fellows keep the stroke! "

" For God's sake, keep up, Johnny! We're coming, Johnny! You keep up a *minnit!* " It was the roller's voice, and it cracked under a sob. Johnny bawled back: " *I'm* all right. He's quiet as a kitten—I'll duck you if you dast to stir! "

But Knute did not stir; and when they had pulled him into the boat, he lay with neither breath nor quiver, and Johnny (towed at the stern to lighten the boat) gave animated orders according to his experience. " He's breathing all right, but tilt his head and get the water out of him—now work his arms and rub him. Get his flask out of his pocket and give him a taste—there, I told you he was all right!"

"He's coming to," bawled the roller. "Say, what if he makes a break?"

"He won't," said Johnny; "but sit on his head if he does."

Knute, however, was like a man stunned, making no resistance, and meekly consenting to be put in a hack, with his two friends, and driven home.

"I make you lots of trouble, boys," he murmured in apology.

"Yes, you do," returned the roller, severely, "and you like to have drownded Johnny! I couldn't swim, or else you'd have drownded me, too. Now, what I want to know is: Are you going to try this d—— trick again?"

The Swede had been smiling feebly, but at the words some sinister memory burned in his melancholy eyes.

"I don't know. I can't tell. I got so much troubles."

"No trouble's so bad you can't bear it like a man," said Johnny. He felt something tugging at his heart, something that hurt it, yet lifted it. He had never felt that way before;

THEY PULLED HIM INTO THE BOAT.

and suddenly he, too, remembered, and added, humbly, "especially if you have good friends."

"And a good wife," added the roller with increased severity. "I've no doubt she's scared to death about you this minute—and so's mine about me. I bet she's been to the grocery, ringing up the Edgewater to know if there's been an accident, or Sam Swift has been hurt. Say, what was that letter you mailed——"

Knute sat up with a spring. "Can't dot man drive faster?" he cried; "I yust remember I tole my vife——"

"I only hope she hasn't run out to catch you herself; and we can't find her," was the roller's dismal augury. "Poor thing! I guess she's 'most crazy."

But he prodded Johnny's side with his elbow and bestowed on him a furtive smile, implying that he secretly regarded Mrs. Larsen's fright with satisfaction.

Knute sank back on the seat; and the roller eyed his troubled countenance and nodded, until his good-nature prompted some homely consolation. "I guess you'll understand each other better after this, Knute. It's going to come out all right."

Johnny sat in his wet clothes and shivered. The night was turning chill, after the terrible day. His exhilaration, which was no more than the effervescence of peril, was all gone, he felt cold in his heart; and his one longing was to make an excuse to jump out of the hack and run. "No, you don't, Johnny Burke," he kept saying to himself, "get a brace on you!" But he choked and went white when the carriage stopped. He opened the door and sprang out, first. He was aware of a pretty cottage and of red geraniums, and a plank walk—but then, he staggered and grew faint, for it was her face flying toward them.

She flung herself into the carriage door. "Tell me first, I'll tell her," she began in a tone like ice; she was pale but she was not screaming or fainting, except that she gasped and suddenly broke into a little choking laugh as she saw Knute.

"Oh, Knute, how could you?" she cried. "Elly's so frightened, she went to the police, herself, to beg them look for you; she's just come back—Elly, Knute's all right!"

The other woman, who looked like Dora, but was not Dora, the woman whose picture he had seen, had passed Johnny and was sobbing in Knute's arms.

"You get him into the house and get off his wet clothes, soon's you can, ma'am," said the roller, who rose to the level of the situation with the ripe composure of a ten years married man. "I'll explain to Miss Glenn how you come to have a husband here, instead of in the Mississippi." The single glimpse Johnny had of the faces of husband and wife as she drew him into the house, assured him that whatever the trouble between them, it had shrivelled out of knowledge in the terror and anguish of the last hour. "She loves him," Johnny thought reverently; and with the thought came another under which he leaned quickly against the side of the porch. "He's weak with his exertions," explained the roller, "and no wonder. Let me tell you—" Johnny was obliged to sit down while the roller depicted the scene in such vivid colors that he did not know his own experience. "Knute's a giant, and he struggled awfully —my—my gracious! my heart was in my mouth, I thought he'd pull him under; but Johnny was calm as if he was in a ball-room— look here, excuse me, I haven't introduced him to you; I *am* rattled, that's a fact. Miss Glenn, Mr. Burke."

"I know Mr. Burke well," she said, "he's a friend of mine." She held out her hand, her beautiful white hand, smiling. But, suddenly, her lips quivered and the tears rose to her eyes. "Oh, I haven't thanked you!" she said, "I *can't*. How brave you are!" Dimly Johnny realized that she was looking at him as she had never looked at him, before.

The roller sent his eyes from one young face to the other; and a smile slowly dawned on his features. "Well, Miss Dora," said he, pleasantly, "I guess I'll be going, my wife's waiting. Don't hurry, Johnny." And he walked away, whistling.

At the street corner he cast a glance behind. The two young figures were still standing, bathed in the enchanted glow of sunset, and Johnny was still holding the girl's hand.

THE "SCAB"

THE "SCAB"

THE train was rolling its huge wheels over the Illinois prairies, not so swiftly as car-wheels are used to roll over that level stretch between Joliet and Chicago; but the day was the third of July, 1894, and there was enough chance that there had been tampering with the rails to excuse caution. It was so warm that most of the car-windows were open; nevertheless in the last car (not a Pullman) the air was heavy with the sickly pungency of apples and orange peel and the indescribable odor of cinders. Dust was everywhere; vibrating in the sunshine that changed its dingy motes into gold, painting the window-ledges gray, and coating the red plush of the seats, except where two commercial travellers had fended off the warm prickle by newspapers. Flies buzzed through the car, and one especial fly so annoyed the younger of the travellers that he chased him to his death, remarking, "There! I wish you were Debs!"

"Debs isn't to blame for the weather or the flies," criticised the other man; "you better be thankful we're going at all. I guess they will have the Rock Island tied up as tight as a drum to-morrow."

"Then I shall wish all the more Debs was this fly!" returned the first man, coolly, slipping into his seat.

"I'm not so blooming certain we can get through, to-day," the other continued; "did you know we have got a scab fireman on?"

"That's why those rocks flew at Spring Valley!"

"They *were* rocks, then?"

"Why, certainly—" Then the speaker's voice sank, to the discomfiture of the elderly woman from the country, two seats in front, who vainly tilted her plump neck backward and strained her ears to catch more than vagrant phrases.

She was a comely old woman, whose gray hair was not thin, whose skin had a wholesome clearness, and whose bright brown eyes sparkled behind her glasses. There was a kind of vigorous neatness about her old-fashioned toilet. She was the single person in the car who was not dusty. As she listened, an emotion not akin to timidity, stirrred the lines of her mouth, and a color not due to the heat, mottled her still pretty cheeks. Rising, she brushed the full folds of her black alpaca skirts with a determined action. She smoothed out the wrinkles of her basque at the waist. With the same brisk and almost angry movements she pulled her antique black straw bonnet off the rack, unswathed it from a blue *barège* veil and tied it firmly on her head. This done, she ran a careful eye over the neat pile of her belongings on the opposite seat, pushed the handbox, covered with wall-paper, into a safer position, rested a portly, greenish-black umbrella against her knee, and sat upright, as one prepared for action.

When the big brakeman, whom every traveller on No. 2 likes, entered with his watercan, she beckoned to him. There had been an interchange of courtesies and fried chicken between the two already; hence he halted with the smile of an acquaintance. "Well, grandma?" said the brakeman.

"Say, you set down by me, cayn't you? I got something to tell you. But I don't want to take you off your business; come back if you ain't got the time now."

Lyon is the most amiable man on the road; he dropped into the seat beside her at once. "It's fifteen minutes to the next station," said he, "and we're running awful light—not twenty passengers on this train. Think of that for the day before the Fourth!"

"It's a shame," agreed the old woman, warmly. "Say"—her voice, which was so mellow and leisurely in its intonations that even its angry tones rang pleasantly, sank into a whisper—"them men behind—don't look round!—the one with the bald head and the big ears and the fat one in the blue striped shirt; they bin settin' all round the car, sheddin' papers wherever they set; and I bin readin' the papers. Why on airth don't the guvernment put a stop to this foolishniss?"

"I guess they won't let 'em upset any more cars," said the brakeman.

"They *better!* Why, it's ridiclous! They throwed stuns at one car, it says. S'posin' there'd bin babies in that car! I got a little grandchild two years old I come nigh a-bringin' with me—how'd I felt if I had! And I guess there's plenty other grandmothers 'sides me, with childern, a-travellin'! Them men say, too, we may have trouble 'cause we got a scab fireman on board; have we?"

"IT'S A SHAME," AGREED THE OLD WOMAN, WARMLY.

The brakeman nodded.

"Do tell! Would you mind tellin' me, jest to oblige, what a scab reely is?"

The brakeman had a round, cheerful young face, to which the freckles only imparted an additional friendliness of expression; but at these artless words it clouded; his lower jaw dropped and he hitched his blue trousers up at the knee, appearing to ask aid of the thick shoes, which were tapping the floor.

"A scab?" said the brakeman, "why, a scab's a feller that scabs—takes another feller's job!"

"Well, but," insisted the countrywoman, "I don't understand. My daughter that I bin visitin' in Iowa, she was havin' a cellar made— and the mason that was doin' it had a man workin' for him that bin workin' for him thirteen year and was the best man he had, but he wasn't a union man, and the boss of the union told him he'd got to send that man off 'cause he didn't belong to the union, or else all the others would strike on him, and they'd boycott him with his customers, so he done it, and another man took his place, now I s'pose *he* was a scab?"

"Didn't they give the feller the choice of joinin' the union?"

"I don't know. I know he went off, and he felt awful bad, 'cause he said 'twasn't no fun huntin' a job this year. Was that man who took his place a scab?"

"Oh, no, ma'am, he was all right, he belonged to the union——"

"Ain't nobody got a right to work without he belongs to the union?"

"That ain't the point—ladies don't understand. It's like this way in a strike: all the workingmen win if the strike wins, and it is thought to be about the durndest mean act a man can do to step in and take the place of some feller who is out really fighting for *him*, see?"

"No, I *don't* see. What good would it 'a' done that mason if the masons had struck, when they wouldn't let anybody hire him anyhow? I don't see no harm in scabs. What's this one's name? Is he a nice man?"

No one is less of an agitator than Jerry Lyon; in preference to argument he answered her questions; Yes, the fireman was a nice man, and his name was Eli Pauls.

"Will they try to hurt us 'cause he's on,

think? Ditch the train maybe, or some sich deviltry—they do them things right along it says in the papers."

"I don't believe the strikers do, railroad boys ain't so mean as that."

"But somebody might—it's done; and if there should be an accident, I hate to trouble you, but I got a daughter-in-law, a widder, lives right in Blue Island—her name's Mrs. Lizzie J. Gayter—and I guess you better send the body, *there*."

"No you don't, grandma," said the brakeman. "I ain't goin' to let you git killed, nor anybody else. That's positive. Don't you believe what those drummers say!"

He went away, laughing, but his face darkened before he met the conductor on the platform.

The conductor was reading a yellow slip of paper.

"Well?" said Lyon, taking an easy, railway pose on the steps.

"They stoned the last train at Blue Island and nearly killed the engineer. Dragged him and the fireman off the cab. Arnold was there with the injunction yesterday afternoon, and they simply hooted him—hollered 'To h—— with the Government,' and tore down the injunctions. He tried to move the trains; but they knocked him down and pounded him. The deputies ran. Nice show for Pauls, ain't it?"

The brakeman pushed his cap back off his curly fair hair, looking the other way. "Pauls has got a wife and six kids," said he, irrelevantly, "and he's been out of work 'most three months he told me. He was stationary engineer for a company that failed. One of his kids is sick; he's worried about him."

"What sort of fellow is he?"

"Oh, he's one of these kinder rabbit men, been dodging around in his cab all the way, 'fraid of stones. He says his wife used to be a school-teacher, but she took in sewing and washing, too, to earn money while he was out of a job. He worked out poll-taxes or anything else he could get—seems they are trying to pay for a house, and he's awful anxious to earn money."

"You ever see his wife?"

"Nah, but he's got a picture of his wife and three of the kids; he wears it in his shirt-pocket. It's got paper over it to keep it clean.

She's a real nice-looking woman, and the kids are nice-looking, too."

"Shaw!" said the conductor; but the exclamation was one of sympathy, and the brakeman so understood it. He rubbed one foot over the other, as he continued, with an affectation of indifference, "Look here, Doughty, suppose I go in and fire for that feller. Max won't mind. Everything is so topsy-turvy now, rules don't count. And all the boys know me, and they won't catch on to him if he's braking in my place. What do you say?"

The conductor was a Scotchman. He rubbed his sandy hair a full minute, saying nothing. Finally, he answered, "Let's go talk to Max, and—you better take my gun!"

They found the engineer, a sun-burned, stolid man, leaning out of his cab, and smoking, while he watched a little crowd of men on the platform.

The fireman busied himself in polishing off a stray stain on some brass-work. He had a nervous air. As he worked his straight, fair hair fell over his red face. He looked up eagerly at Lyon's approach. "What's the news, Mr. Lyon?" said he.

"What's the news, Jerry?" said the engineer.

"Nothing good," answered Lyon. "Say, Pauls, I guess you will attract less observation from our excitable friends, braking in a quiet, peaceful way than firing. Let's exchange jobs the rest of the trip to Chicago!"

The fireman flushed. "No, you don't," said he, "I ain't much on fighting, maybe, but I won't have another man stoned in my place!"

"I could have told you he wouldn't let you," said Max, the engineer, in his emotionless, bass voice.

Lyon's persuasions availed nothing, and he was forced to leave Pauls at the furnace, grumbling as he went.

But had he realized how much lighter was the fireman's heart as he peered over the grates at the saw of flame behind the smudge, he had felt less need to belabor his own stupidity for making "a bad break" for nothing. For, at that very moment Pauls was swallowing hard, yearning in his soul for some future chance to pound a possible assailant of Lyon's to a jelly, and inaudibly praising Lyon to his wife. "I do think the boys are beginning to get used to me a bit," says Pauls, choking. A little kindness went a long way with the "scab." He was a quiet man, not prone to vanity nor to take offence, who had rehearsed to himself in advance the snubs and annoyances that a "scab" must count on getting, and had promised himself not to resent them. Julie couldn't understand; but he, himself, had the workingman's feeling about the man who would steal another man's job. He didn't blame the yardmen and the train crews taking his presence in bad part and showing their resentment in any form short of stones. "It's natural," Pauls used to say rather drearily to himself, folding his bare arms on the window-sill of the cab and puffing at his pipe; "they don't like me taking Ridgely's place. *I* don't think I'm wrong. The strike is a fool strike and a mean one, and Ridgely hasn't got any right to throw up his job and then expect other men to let their families suffer rather than take it from him. Julie's right. I owe more to her and the children than I do to a man I never saw in my life. But I can't expect the boys that knew Ridgely to look at it like I do!"

And Pauls had so much of the workingman's prejudice in him that he felt cowed by the tacit disapproval of his comrades; he could not keep his chin in the air did the street boys yell "Scab!" at him. A workingman's comrades are his society, there is no public opinion to him outside his own class; to lose the good-will of the men who work at his side, every day, is to be an outcast. It had really taken more moral courage for Pauls to climb up the steps of the cab, the first time, than many a man needs during his whole life. "I ain't doing wrong, if they do think so," he said, doggedly. But he felt grateful even for the cool indifference of his new comrades. "They haven't done a mean thing to me," he told Julie, and he was very cheerful before her and the little sick boy who was interested in the engine. He didn't tell his wife how often he thought of Ridgely, the striking fireman. There was his oil-can and the bits of waste that he had used in polishing the engine; sombrely enough Pauls stared at them many a time, wondering what manner of man Ridgely was, and if he needed the place. Once he asked Max whether Ridgely was a married man, and stuck his head into the furnace door and withdrew it, red as the fire inside.

"No," said Max. He added no possible romance for Ridgely. Pauls heaved a mighty shovelful of slack on the grates. "What kind of a man was Ridgely?" said he, coughing in the dust that he raised. But Max did not notice his confusion and answered carelessly, "Oh, he wasn't much 'count. He didn't keep things clean, and he was always getting tired shovelling and wanting to run the engine!"

And then the conductor had happened to come up; and Pauls had never got his courage into action again. Not even to Lyon who was kind to him, could he unpack his wishes and scruples and regrets about Ridgely. Max was kind to him, also; but Max was a taciturn man who smoked a short pipe, consuming his thoughts, as some chimneys consume their smoke. Lyon, on the contrary, was an open-hearted, frank fellow, reared on a farm in a large family, who insensibly began to pity Pauls as soon as he knew that he had six children. He was not aware that he was kind—indeed, he regarded his behavior as having the happy mixture of forbearance and contempt due from a loyal member of a union that was not striking and opposed to the present strike, to a useful but odious "scab." In Pauls's case, however, his feelings were complicated by—Ridgely! None of the train-crew liked Ridgely; and Lyon hated him. Lyon had a sweetheart; and he was bitterly jealous of Ridgely, with his handsome face and fluent tongue. Ridgely had bragged that he could marry "Jerry Lyon's best girl, any time he wanted to," and Lyon's fists clinched whenever he thought of the man. But he couldn't abuse him to Pauls; so Pauls wondered at the silence. To-day, Ridgely was persistently in his mind. Was poor Ridgely among the rioters? "I'd like to do that man a good turn!" thought Pauls.

"Next stop is Blue Island," said Max.

"They are quiet enough, here," said Pauls, looking out at the pretty little houses with their fresh paint and the dusty street, and a gray team of farm-horses with a farmer at their heads. The farmer, seeing that his horses would stand, left them and approached the train. Pauls saw his face light up, and in a second saw him swing himself on the platform of the rear car.

"Yes, it's quiet enough, here," said Max.

"But I see some white ribbons," said Pauls. "Don't it seem an awful strange thing that a week ago we were all so peaceful and now maybe there'll be civil war."

"There won't be no civil war," said Max; "those fellers won't fight; it's jest a big bluff."

"Well, I hope so," said Pauls, stealing a glance at the contemptuous immobility of the engineer's face; "I'd hate to kill a man, it would be an awful thing; and yet—I guess I'd do it before I'd give up and let 'em kill the engine. What do you think?"

Max's peaceful face did not change; but he put his hand to his hip-pocket and showed a hammerless revolver. "I ain't going to let them kill *my* engine if I can help it," said he, quietly. "They'd hurt her. They don't mind what they do to an engine, those fellers." He flicked a speck off the shining brass-work.

"She's a beauty," acquiesced Pauls, "it would hurt me, too, to see her hurt."

A faint gleam crept into Max's gray eyes. "Ridgely used to say she wasn't no better'n half a dozen engines on the road," said he. "I—I ain't sorry Ridgely's gone."

Pauls essayed to speak lightly, but his voice shook, "Well, I—fact of the matter is, I've felt pretty bad 'bout taking his place."

"You needn't," said Max.

He said no more, either because he would

not have said more, in any event, or because he saw three men under the cab-window.

The three men were Lyon, the conductor, and the farmer. An air of controlled agitation hung about them all. The conductor spoke in a low voice, plainly trying to seem unconcerned. He said, "They have been having a h—— of a time in Blue Island and Chicago, all day!" Now, the conductor was a Presbyterian who never used an oath.

"So?" said Max.

"Don't look as if anything was up," said Doughty, rapidly; "there's no knowing who's spying on us. I'll explain to you." He explained in a few sentences. The man with them was the son of a lady on the train. He lived about two miles out of Blue Island, and he had gone in early, to be there to meet his mother, who was coming to visit him. He had a sister in town, and she had seen the rioters dropping something between the rails. No doubt they were spiking the switches, but they hadn't driven the spikes in. She told her brother, and he had gone to the next town to meet his mother there and to warn the train. The place was a little before they entered the depot. "That's the situation, boys," said

Doughty, " and I don't know how you feel about it, but I said, with Max at the éngine I believed we could run the train into Chicago, and I don't like to be downed."

"What you think of doing?" asked Max, cutting off a slice of tobacco.

Doughty and the farmer exchanged glances. "We are not going to do much of anything, I guess, but Mrs. Gayter, this gentleman's mother, says those bolts must be picked up, unsuspected, and she is game to do it for us, herself. She has a plan—well, I guess we cooked it up amongst us. But the old lady will dress up in an old dress she's got with her, and be a peanut-woman. We can get all Tommy's peanuts and apples. And when she gets to the spot she will tip her basket over and while she is picking them up, she will pick up a few spikes that are of no account round there. The old lady is smart as a whip-lash and I believe she will do it."

"But somebody ought to go with her!" Pauls cried, " somebody that knows about the road——"

The conductor took the words off his tongue, "Lyon, of course, spoke up for the job, but I told him they would be on to *him* in a flash."

"But they don't know *me*," said Pauls.

"Well, if you want the job, I guess Lyon can fire for you," returned the conductor. "Come on back into the car."

Pauls followed. Lyon at the door looked back at the engineer. "Will he do, guess?" said he.

"Sure," said Max.

Ten minutes later, Max and Lyon looked out of the cab-window to see a farm-wagon disappear through a radiant cloud of dust. Pauls sat behind drilling the impromptu peanut-woman in her part.

Her son had brought a bit of white ribbon, which he insisted on pinning to her blue calico gown, on the shoulder (this was her stipulation), where she would not need to see it. She had pulled a stiff and very clean yellow sun-bonnet over her head. "'Tis pretty warm, this bunnit, but I'm willin' to do my part to put down the rebellion," said she, stoutly. "My father fit for the flag in 1812 and my husband was killed for it in 1863, leavin' Sam, there, no more'n a baby; and I'm willin' to bear my testimony, now. Talk of persentiments, I felt a persentiment creepin' cole down my spine, the minnit I heard them men a-talkin'. And I got all my things ready, straight, I didn't have to keep Sam waitin', none!"

Her high spirits, which were not in the least feigned, put a new fire into Paul's veins. He had not thought of the matter in such a light. "Every good American ought to be helpin', now," cried she; "it's a good way, I guess, of celebratin' the Fourth!"

"That's so," her son agreed, smiling on her proudly. But for the most part he was very grave, having a better appreciation than she of the quality of the scene to which he was taking her. Pauls did not see the houses nor the parched woodlands, nor the trampled, scorched roadside drifting past his wide eyes; he saw a tiny lawn, green and closely clipped, he saw the clematis vine on a cottage porch, rustling and waving in the wind, and through the purple and green he saw a patched hammock with a little, smiling, pale face on the pillow, and a black-haired woman rocking and sewing, near. He remembered some verses that he had learned once to speak in school, they were about a dying gladiator,

"There were his young barbarians all at play,
There was their Dacian mother."

Suppose those Blue Island toughs killed him,

would *he* see Julie and Jim and the girls? The farmer half turned his head. "Got a pistol?" said he.

Pauls shook his dead. "They cost so much," said he, apologetically. "I was a stationary engineer, before, and didn't need one. Max asked me if I had one, but I knew he would want to give me his, and he needed it, so I said, 'That's all right;' and he thought I had one."

"I wish I had one," said the farmer, with a rueful smile, "but I haven't anything—except cannon firecrackers for my children!"

"They're better'n nothin'," observed the old woman, cheerily. "Look, Sam, ain't we comin' into Blue Island?"

Pauls stared down the straggling sky line of shops and houses. He could see the street jammed with black figures, wavering in ragged lines; he saw, here and there, a spiral of smoke curling up from the open street; that must be a blockaded engine. But, in general, the sky was strangely pure, no smoke from the great factories, no smoke from the railroad-shops. "Debs has kept his word," explained Sam; "he's tied the Rock Island up tight."

Their plans were now to be tested. Sam

drew up the wagon close to the wooden sidewalk, where a patch of smart-weed and jimson made a squalid boulevard between the road and the planks. He kissed his mother, saying, "I'll keep close behind, ma, mind that!" Then he shook Pauls's hand. Pauls said, "It's Mrs. W. T. Pauls, if you lose the address." Sam nodded. "And you look after your mother, don't mind *me*, whatever happens," said Pauls. Then he crossed the street and strolled along, an idle stranger, seeking the spectacles of the day. On the other side, an old peanut-woman proffered her wares to the few passers-by. In the middle of the road, a farmer drove a tired team of horses slowly down the broad street. Presently, the stranger, who looked like most of the men about, in his flannel shirt and shabby trousers, had come to the railway tracks and the crowd. An observable thing about the crowd was its youth. There were beardless young fellows at every turn. They perched on fences and car-roofs. Their hats were pushed back on their heads, their faces were flushed, and they called jeers and witty abuse of the marshals (as they esteemed wit) from one group to another. Some of them walked the rounds of the trains, and stared at the weary faces at the windows. Another feature of the crowd was the number of women and children in its ranks, so that the wailing of children was one of the component parts of the din. The women were untidy of dress, as plainly in their working-clothes as the men were in theirs, their tousled hair often uncovered and their faces disfigured by a fury of excitement. Not a tin star was in sight; but a policeman leaned drowsily against a saloon-door and looked to be in a Nirvana of rest amid the turmoil.

The shabby man walked along the tracks just behind the wagon. Though the way was clear the wagon halted for a second, as if to allow the driver to read one of the placards on the cars. It went on and the man, following, stood still for the same purpose. He was roused by an exclamation of distress, in a woman's pipe. Behold, behind him, the unlucky peanut-woman who had stumbled and spilled her nuts over the track! The children, swarming there as everywhere, were on all fours after them in a trice; and the owner crawled about the rails, lamenting and picking up peanuts. The man seemed to be a good-natured fellow, for he was active in dispersing the small banditti and collecting peanuts. He did not lose patience with the old woman, although she thriftily gathered up the last peanut from the frogs and once or twice in her eagerness caught her cotton gown between the cunning joints, requiring his help to release her. " Good-by, grandma," he called, as she stumbled painfully away, and disappeared in the crowd. He remained, studying the placards. He brought some food from a restaurant to a woman in one of the cars. He joined in one or two very brief conversations. He watched a pleasant-looking countrywoman in a black alpaca gown (who came out of one of the better class of houses down a side-street) clamber into the countryman's wagon. She looked about her, smiling happily like a child; and he smiled, too.

But, immediately, his mouth compressed itself in a very different smile. And he walked up the track.

The train ran into Blue Island, as if the rails were eggs. Max with his hand on the lever, did not let his glance swerve a hair's-breadth. Big drops rolled down Lyon's pale face, his teeth flashed in a grin of intensest excitement and watchfulness; he kept his eyes on Max, who, except for his keen eyes, looked as impassive as ever.

"We were to stop if we didn't see him," said Lyon.

"There he is," said Max—he spoke as quietly as he would have spoken ten days before—"yes, that's him. He's signalling for us to go straight on and not stop. Does he know the signals, for sure?"

"Yes, I taught him. By —— Look at him; do you see the mob?"

"Do you hear them? Boys this looks bad!"—it was a new voice; Doughty, the conductor, had made his way to the engine, he was clambering along the foot-board.

"Get in, Doughty," said Max, not turning his head, "I hear them. We're getting near."

Near enough, now, for the three men to hear the hollow roar and hiss as one word was screamed by hundreds of throats, "Scab! scab!" Near enough to see the furious faces, the clinched fists and the women's arms scratching in the common insult of the mob. And near enough to see, on a pile of lumber, a single man, his arms above his head waving the signal. "*Track clear! Don't stop!*"

"He knows they'll block the track. It's

"TRACK CLEAR! DON'T STOP!"

our only chance to get through," said the conductor.

"Scabs! Scabs! Kill the scabs! Pull 'em off the engine!" a woman's voice shrieked, shriller than the rest.

"He's going to make a run for us," cried Lyon; "that's Slippery Dick behind him; they've caught on to the signals—yah, I knew it, there come the stones!"

"He ain't running to us, he's running 'cross the street!" said Max, "he won't bring trouble on us."

"Here's another stone," said the conductor; "I must get back to my passengers. Max, you know the orders. Let her go!"

Lyon thought he heard a queer sound from Max when he pushed the lever and opened the throttle. "I hate to leave that fellow!" he growled; but the great black bulk quivered and raced down on the mob, faster at each word. The slack flew into the furnace. Then, the fireman's head pitched out of the black dust and he stole a glance through the window.

"Nobody ever kept her so clean like he did!" Max was muttering. "Jerry, can't you see nothing?"

Lyon shook his fist in an ecstasy of rage.

"If there wasn't a whole litter of children in the way I'd shoot, I would by ——! D—— them, they're stoning him! That dirty—Bully for grandma, she's trying to get him in the wagon— Oh!—" Lyon swore in a sob of passion that cracked into a fierce laugh.

"Why don't you tell, instead of hollering like a wild Injun?" cried the justly exasperated Max. "You know I can't turn 'round!"

"It was that black-hearted devil, Dick," said Lyon; "he hit the old lady with a coupling-pin, tumbled her clean off the seat, and Pauls smashed him with the same pin— They've got him down— Oh, Max, I cayn't stand—rrh!"

It was no articulate exclamation that reeled out of Lyon's lips, but rather a gasp, a groan, and a scream all jumbled together. And Max heard nothing of it, for even that modern Roman sentinel wheeled round the upper part of him at a tremendous barking clatter of explosion, followed by a tumult of shrieks and shouts.

"I think that must have been a bomb," said Lyon, in a small, gentle voice.

"What can you see?" asked Max, a statue again.

"They all seem to be running—the horses are running, too—I can't see——"

Nor could he, for there was nothing to be seen but a lessening perspective of cars and rails; nothing to be heard but the pounding gallop of the insensate steed that hurried them away.

"I'm going back to Blue Island on the street-cars, the minit I git to Chicago," Lyon announced. "I'm going to see about that bomb! Poor Pauls."

"That didn't sound to me so much like a bomb, it sounded just like cannon firecrackers," meditated Max.

Nor was it a bomb. When Pauls ran he had no thought to run to his friends. He was simply trying to turn the attention of the mob away from the engine.

But thus running, he heard a voice, "Here, here! climb in!" And he saw the wagon beside him. The next instant, the old woman dropped. There was blood on her gray hair, and Pauls's brain seemed to burst into flames. He struck furiously at the assailant, and as if by the wind of his own blow was felled.

He did not feel hurt nor frightened, he only felt a mad, overwhelming brute longing to fight, to kill, before they should trample the life out of him! But then the crash and the blaze came; and the crowd was running and he was lying on his back, stupidly staring up into the sky. He squinted one eye along the ground until it encountered a curl of red paper, and he began to laugh. Firecrackers or not, some people were hurt, for he had heard the screams. And he laughed again, while he crawled to his feet. A woman—not a woman of the crowd, a woman with a neat dress and smooth hair—ran to him and helped him along, urging him to haste. She took him into a drug-store where they washed his face and dosed him with brandy and got him into another coat.

"The lady in the wagon—does anybody know if the lady in the wagon was hurt?" Pauls begged, the instant they let his mouth alone.

"Ma?" cried the kind woman beside him, "ma's all right, just round the corner in the wagon. I'll take you."

She guided him out of the house, by the back door, and down a peaceful alley to a shady street where the Gayter wagon stood under a branching maple, the horses nibbling grass as tranquilly as if they had never sniffed powder and known war.

Mrs. Gayter sat on the front seat. Except the flutter of a white handkerchief beneath the generous curve of her bonnet, not a mark of combat showed on her genial visage. Sam wore a new hat and he had a bruise on his cheek-bone, but he, too, was smiling; and he wrung Pauls's hand in a mighty grip.

"*Did* you kill him?"

"I don't know," replied Pauls, "I did my best!"

Sam looked downcast, but Mrs. Gayter's rich tones struck in, consolingly, "Maybe it's best not. I don't wish no feller-cretur to be killed. Don't feel bad, boys. He gave me a reel good chance to set off that hull bunch of firecrackers, and I reely think, besides, I run over him. We hadn't orter be too ha'sh! Mr. Pauls, there's one thing, though, I wish you'd do for me, that is, git some firecrackers in Chicago for the childern, the king firecrackers. I cayn't git them here, and the childern would be so disapp'inted if they didn't git 'em. Sam will come in here for them to-morrow mornin' and Lizzie will show you what cars to take."

Lizzie showed Pauls so well that without further misadventure he reached the city and ran into Max and Lyon, just starting out in search of him. He thought it was worth the tussle and all his bruises to have Lyon wring his hand and Max grin placidly upon him. "Well, they didn't kill you," said Max. "Did you kill Ridgely?"

"Me? Ridgely?" repeated Pauls, dazed.

"That was Ridgely hit the old lady," explained Lyon. "Slippery Dick Ridgely—used to run with us."

"Was that man Ridgely?" said Pauls, with a deep sigh. "Boys, I've been sorry for him——"

"You needn't be!" said Max, grimly.

"I wish you'd killed him!" said Lyon.

"I did my best," said Pauls, humbly. "At least"—he added the words with a queer smile that only Max understood—"at least if I haven't killed him, I've killed his ghost!"

THE CONSCIENCE OF A
BUSINESS MAN

THE CONSCIENCE OF A BUSINESS MAN

A SMALL cyclone was blowing through the eight-inch mill of the Edgewater Steel Works. Sam Swift, the roller, commonly a mild and taciturn man, had been exasperated to the swearing point (which, in truth, is easy to reach in a rolling-mill!) by the persistent and heart-breaking stupidity of his finisher. The last offence was to forget to grease the hole, causing the oval iron to stick, so that when the roller impatiently clapped his tongs to it, it was beyond a giant's muscles, and Swift had pulled it out of the guides, cursing. "Yesterday you tangled up the ovals, and to-day you forget the grease," he raged. "You're the worst man to poke in iron I ever did see! Blank! blank!! blank!!!"—the finisher taking it all with exemplary patience, and Swift, amid his swelling fury, not losing a second, but rapidly and effectively pushing a new oval into the guides.

Finally the finisher opened his lips, but not to defend himself. He said, meekly, " Say, Sam, there's the kid and Mr. Jamieson and the old man coming our way, right behind you."

Sam remarked that he didn't care if the devil were coming; but it was one thing to swear at his finisher, himself, quite another to expose him to censure from the higher powers, and he subsided into a resentful silence.

Young Randall, the secretary, came first, a pleasant, cool figure, that steaming August day, in white crash, with a pink rose in his buttonhole. Next, Mr. Martin Jamieson, the treasurer, middle-aged, meagre, rather nearsighted, never knowing any of the men; and last, was the president, " the old man." Rivers was his name—Jabez Wentworth Rivers. He always signed it J. W. Rivers. He was of middle stature and full habit, and when moved to anger (which was oftener than was good for his soul) he would grow very red in the face. Randall, who had inherited his father's stock, and was but recently graduated from Harvard, considered his senior to be lacking in dignity. Secretly, also, he feared that Rivers's business talents had been overrated. He was too cautious; he did not perceive business possi-

AND TOLD HIM HOW THE GREAT HOUSE HAD BEEN HIS GRANDFATHER'S.

bilities quickly. Randall said as much to Jamieson once; that was in the spring, and Jamieson had answered grimly, "This is no year for branching out; the old man is right." To-day, Randall thought Jamieson was telling the truth. His eye wandered to the dinner-buckets that were coming into the mill.

"If we shut down what will they have to put in them?" he questioned, and his face darkened. He did not notice Swift smiling and nodding.

The roller's face fell. "Can't be he's mad at me for anything," he thought. "Oh, I guess he's jest busy thinking." He liked the secretary—all the men liked him, he was so sunny and good-natured, and remembered their given names.

The old man rolled in, looking much as usual, finding time to stop and mutter over some ovals a fraction too small (nobody else would have noticed them; they were accepted by an amiable inspector, without kicking, the next week), and to nod at Swift in passing. But the roller looked after him and shook his head. The old man was aging, or else something had gone wrong; he didn't have that drawn twitch about his mouth last week. At noon the heater of the twelve-inch mill sauntered up to Swift. He was a man who picked up all the shop gossip. "Hear they're going to shet down, Monday," he remarked.

"H——!" said the roller.

"Yes, sir; orders give out—folks won't specify. Waiting till after election, they say."

"Who told you?"

"Nev' mind; I ain't giving it away. Say, did you mind how glum the kid was?"

"What if he was?"

"That's what. He thinks it an all-fired shame, and so 'tis. Say, I got five children, oldest ain't 'leven. Mill I was working in last shet down and didn't run for two months. Save anything? How'n h—— kin I save anything, me in that fix? I tell you, Sammy, it's all wrong, jest like the kid says—I heard him talking to some girls he was taking over the works—our hull industrial system is wrong, says he. You bet your life it is, too! Look at old Rivers, s'posing they do shet down, 'twon't faze him. He'll be making a little less money, that's all; but you'n me will be skinning round for credit at the grocer and figurin' how often a week we dast have meat!"

"I guess it won't be precisely a picnic to

Jabez Rivers," said the roller, mildly, as became a conservative and " better fixed " man. The roller had saved money; neither was he so rich in the poor man's joys as the other.

" Lemme tell you something. What do you think of a man who's going to spend forty or fifty thousand dollars buying a house while men are begging for work to keep their families? That's what he's going to do, and shet down his shops. Do you call that fair dealin' ? "

" He's *got* a house; what do you mean? "

" I know he has—a fine one; that makes it worse. 'Tain't as if he was having to pay rent. No, sir; I know all about it."

" Maybe 'twould ease you a mite to spit it all out, then. What's the old man wanting a fifty-thousand dollar house for? He ain't one of them all-for-show folks. Never was."

The heater extracted a light-brown and slightly crumpled cigar from a pocket, lighted it, and puffed a second under the critical gaze of the roller.

" *Segars!* " commented the roller. " I smoke a pipe, but he with five children and his wife not rugged, he must have his *segar*. Hm! " But this was in silence, and the heater continued, "Why, 'twas like this: The old man come round to the twelve-inch with Jamieson and they were talkin', and I heard him say, 'Yes, I got the cash together, fur '— I don't mind the name—' is after the place, too; but spot cash will be the temptation nobody can resist these days. I can tell you it was rather a job getting it myself, and I guess I sacrificed some things; but I tell you '—and when he got there the old man spoke kinder queer, dretful earnest I call it, and, says he, 'Jamieson, my mind's ben sot on gittin' that house ever sence I was a little shaver, worrying 'cause my mother was setting up nights to knit me mittens. First, I was going to buy it for my mother, then for my wife, and now, I guess it'll end in being for my daughter. That house used to be my grandfather's, and I guess there ain't a living being knows what I feel about gitting it back agin; but when I could buy it, I hadn't the money, and when I got the money the folks that had the house wouldn't sell it; but my chance is come,' says he. Then Jamieson, he mumbled something—he's kinder bloodless feller, Jamieson, you know—and they went away. But I know he's kep' at it. That's why we can't run the shops."

"If they shet down the shops," said Swift, dryly, disdaining to show any impression made on him by the other's narrative, " if they shet down the shops it will be because they can't run them on a profit. Nobody's going to run shops at a loss. *You* wouldn't in the old man's place."

"I wouldn't make my profit out of flesh and blood, I know that much," said the heater, doggedly, " but I know the Rivers tribe, root and branch. They're hard, driving men, I come from Jabez Rivers's town, and my father's seen him when he needed shoes on his feet, too. He needn't talk so big. His father was none too fine a man—got drunk and squandered his money and his ma took in sewing. He'd ought to know how it feels to have your stomach pinched; he's had many a hungry day, I guess, himself. But his grandfather, the old judge, he was a cruel old tyrant; and the old man's a chip of the same block; and he forgets how he was poor himself, and takes it out of the poor man. You'd think he'd sorter want to help a man come from his own town——"

" He did give you a job," said Swift.

" A job! Ain't I give him good work?"

"Well, you're all right when you're steady; but last week when the old man come round I looked to see you git a walking ticket——"

"I was doing my work if I was a bit in liquor!"

"A bit is it? a *good* bit. I seen him squinting his eyes at you, and I could not make out why he turned the other way and never took no notice. I can, now. It's lucky for you you come from the same town."

The townsman sneered, but made no reply, while Swift drank the last swallows of his coffee, and said that his wife certainly did make good coffee.

"I don't expect *my* wife'll have a chance next week to make any coffee, good or bad," was the heater's dismal comment; "but you bet the Riverses won't stint in *their* coffee! I swear I don't think it fair dealing—one man's to git all the good things of living and another, jest's good, to go sweating out his days and glad for a drop of whiskey to forget his misery!"

"If it comes to that, where's the fairness of the Lord's making one man smart and another a poor, shiftless fool, don't know enough to keep a job when he gits it?"

"There ain't so much difference in men's intellecks, if you come to that! It is the way they're treated. It's this present iniquitous industrial servitude which pulls the laboring man down and keeps him down!"

"There ain't sech an awful difference in rich folks' happiness and poor folks'," began Swift, but the heater cut in excitedly, "There is all the difference in the world. Look at me, lost a child with diphtheria, and drinking ever since, 'cause I can't bear the sorrer, and look at him——"

"Yes, look at him! His son Tom, oldest son, died four years ago, this last winter——"

"And the best thing he ever did do," interrupted the heater, with a sneer, "call that a trial?"

"Don't you call it the wust kind of trial that your son's death should be the best thing could happen to him and to you? Well, I do. And then his wife's been dead a good while; and he lost Jabez last summer, a little more'n a year ago. Jabez——" the roller hesitated for a second, adding, in a careful voice, a little dry and higher, "Jabez, he was learning the business, he worked with me, my finisher. He was a mighty nice boy. That's what I called

him—Jabez. And he called me Sam. I've"
—his voice caught on something in his throat
and staggered a little—" I've swore at him
many a time! We were good friends, we
were; and he knew how to take things, and
we'd have our dinners together. My wife always sends me in hot dinners, and Jabez he
liked them lots better than the girly things
they'd be putting into his pail. Jabez had
more pluck than a game rooster. I never saw
a man stand up to it, after he'd been burned,
better'n him! And smart—he was the smart-
est boy ever in these works or anywhere else,
and just as pleasant-tempered and high-prin-
cipled, and the old man set his eyes by him.
They'd ride home every evening, in the bug-
gy, Jabez slouching his back over, for all the
world like the old man. He didn't look much
like him, though. I guess he was the hand-
somest feller ever seen in this town; and when
he wasn't working you'd ought to seen his
clothes. I went to the theatre with him, once.
He was better dressed than the man on the
stage that was playing he was an earl, or some
sech foolishness. The kid is nice looking; but
he ain't in it with Jabez. Don't you call it terrible to lose a son like that?"

The heater admitted that it was hard, but a good deal depended on how much a man felt—the Riverses were always hard as nuts.

"Maybe the old man is and maybe he ain't," said Swift. "I know one thing, he'll never cease mourning for Jabez, till his own time comes. He's showed me—I went up to his house once, he asked me, 'bout some business—he showed me Jabez's certificate that he got to college, all writ in Latin; and he told me some about the boy, what a good boy he was. 'You needn't tell me nothing 'bout that,' says I, 'ain't he worked with me!' I guess I sorter broke down then, I was feeling awful bad myself. The old man and me always seemed to understand each other after that, somehow. He'd come here and stand 'round where Jabez used to work, never saying a word. I'd know he was thinking how Jabez used to look, laughing and hustling about; and I'd want so to say a word and know I couldn't, and feel so—so *damn* I'd have to go off and swear about it to Knute and Johnny, who knew Jabez, too."

The heater thought maybe the old man felt bad; *he'd* "never seen any sign of feeling about any of the Riverses; maybe Sam knew the old man better——"

"Lots better," returned Sam, calmly; "I ought to, seeing I've worked with him going on nine years. The old man has got lots of good things 'bout him. He always keeps his word; and he fights fair." Sam laughed. "That makes me think of the time we struck on him, when I was first working with him. I was one of a deputation foolish enough to try to scare the old man; and by G— he put us out of the window while we were plunging 'round with our pops. I had to laugh, he did it so slick. 'I'll report you to the lodge,' says he; 'you're clean against your own rules and regulations;' and I told the boys we were. So we were, too; the old man was sound. We had a talk, next day, and fixed things up pretty much his way. I didn't suppose he'd noticed me; but, about a week after, there happened to be a job at night rolling and he gave it to me, and in a month he gave me the mill. 'I notice you have a little horse sense, Swift,' says he; 'keep it!' Well, I've tried to. I've seen considerable, off and on, of the old man, and I can tell you, now, he's all right; if there's a show to keep the shops running, they'll run!"

"HE SHOWED ME JABEZ'S CERTIFICATE."

"God knows I hope so," said the heater, with a sigh; "it's terrible times to lose a job. All the same, he'll shet down ruther'n lose money, you say——"

"What's that?" another man asked, catching the sentence as he passed; "you ain't heard the shops was to shet down?"

"He ain't heard nothing, really," Sam struck in curtly; "he's chinning to amuse himself by scaring us."

"My wife's sick, and we've got a new baby, and the doctor prescribes terrible expensive things," said the man, "and we're kinder behind, anyhow. I don't know what we will do if the shops shet down."

A third man came up, wearing an anxious face, and a fourth, a fifth; Sam was glad to hear the whistle.

For half an hour the officers of the Edgewater Steel Works had been talking. Jamieson had explained the business situation. Randall had questioned and added dismal facts concerning orders. But the old man had said little. Lolling ungracefully in his chair, he had listened and attended to his nails with a pen-knife, while Randall shuddered. The president stood little on niceties of manner, where he felt himself at home; and much more than by his own fireside (which his daughter and only living child ruled), did he feel himself at home in his office. Now and then, he would throw a cross-grained sentence at Randall; but, really, he was snubbing the secretary by sheer force of habit; he hardly remembered his own words. What his frowning gray eyes saw was not the handsome oaken woodwork or the gay carpet of the office, but a stately, prim, white mansion, with gambrel roof and porches, and tall white Corinthian columns shining through the elms. He sniffed the pungent fragrance of honeysuckle; he could feel the cool tingle of the moist, plastic earth against a boy's bare feet. Suddenly, his heart stirred with the memory of his mother's voice. When he was only twelve, his mother had shown him the house, one day (but he always had known it), and told him how the great house had been his grandfather's, when his father was a boy. "It will be ours again, sometime," he cried, "you'll see, *I'll* get it for you!"

And, even while they talked, his father had drifted down the street, a little crowd of jeering boys at his heels; and Jabez had flown at

WHAT HIS FROWNING GRAY EYES SAW WAS NOT THE OAKEN WOODWORK OF THE OFFICE.

them like a wild cat. He taunted them as he struck, "You're nothing but common boys, *my* grandfather was a judge; he sent your grandfathers to jail! We used to own that house! I can lick any one of you!" Whereupon, naturally, the boys thumped him, and he was rescued by his mother, bruised and bloodied and (far dolefuller mischance) muddied and torn. "I don't know how I can *ever* mend your pants," sighed the poor woman. It didn't console her that he should repeat, anew, that he would buy the Judge's house for her. When he went to bed, that night, he cried. Then, he resolved to buy the house. He had two things he wanted to do, wanted as bad as a man could want things, he guessed; to buy that house and to see Jabez an officer of the Edgewater. The desolate father looked at Randall across the table. "There's where he'd have sat," he thought; "he knew more in a day than that young blowhard in a year. Yet the boy's got stuff in him, too. Don't you be a dog in the manger, Jabez Rivers! The old Judge would be ashamed of you. How he'd have taken to Jabez—" He shifted his position abruptly; his face with its clean-shaven heavy jaws and beetling eyebrows looked almost savage to Randall at that instant. But Randall was too desperately in earnest, in the plea that he was making, to fear the face of man. His words flowed like lava. "It is an atrocious bargain! we get wealth and soft living and adulation and praise in the newspapers if we are half way decent, and they get—the right to work! Is that a fair bargain? But they don't get even that; when we're making money, if they kick we are ready to call them all sorts of names, but when the pinch comes, we cast them aside, turn them off, won't even give them the poor right to work! I call the civilization that, when the land is groaning with plenty, refuses the man who only asks for work, I call it a failure and a disgrace!"

"Huh!" said Rivers. The sound partook of the nature both of a snort and a grunt.

"We pay the highest market wages, you say; but I say we owe them something more than the bare money we pay them. They are human beings, not machines, and we owe it to them to treat them like human beings, and not take our profits out of their skins."

"We are more likely, if we keep on, to be paying them wages out of ours," said Jamieson, "the question isn't whether the present industrial system is wrong—though I observe that Rivers and I hadn't a penny or a right more than any workingman has, and we have managed under the present iniquity, to get along in the world, but that isn't the question; it is simply whether we can afford to run the Edgewater at a loss for three months."

"Couldn't we try? And"—he flushed up to his eyes but went on sturdily—"I have a few thousands, and perhaps my mother and sister——"

"Huh!" said Rivers, "don't risk women's money!"

"We haven't the right to risk the stockholders' money," said Jamieson, "especially when the chances are we shall lose it. Now, I don't enjoy shutting down the shops any more than you do; but I'm in the steel business to make money; when we stand to lose money I think we better quit."

"But—my own money——"

"It's only a few thousands, and it isn't a few thousands will run this concern between now and November—the banks shut tight as an oyster, and gilt edge paper no use on earth!"

"That's right," said Rivers. He also added, "Huh!"

"Then, you will shut down?" said Randall, turning his pale, fair face, and flashing, excited blue eyes on the president. In spite of his Harvard training he was trembling.

There was an instant's pause; even Jamieson made a grimace.

"I guess we better keep on," said the old man.

"How?" said Jamieson.

"Well, I don't think we ought to risk the money of the concern; nor to pay fancy interest to borrow. Besides, as you say, the banks are all sitting down on their funds. But I have some money of my own, forty or fifty thousand. I'll let you have that, taking the risks and the profits—if there are any, myself. And we'll keep running until election, anyhow. How's that?"

Randall caught his breath, his hand which was impulsively outstretched to Rivers, dropped as he met the old man's keen and chilly glance. He sat silent and felt dizzy.

"But," faltered Jamieson, "I understood you meant—there was another purpose——"

"I've changed my mind," the old man interrupted, sharply; "I'll be obliged if you'll leave that out."

"Why, certainly," agreed Jamieson, nervously. He hesitated; he confessed to Randall, later, that he was of a mind to shake hands with the old man himself; but did not judge his aspect propitious, therefore he compromised with his feelings by drawing a cigar from his case and offering it, remarking: " Yes, Mr. Rivers, that will be a very nice way out, and we are very much obliged; and I'm sure the men will be relieved. Well, I am relieved myself; it's infernally unpleasant shutting down. And then, there are the furnaces. Then, it's decided. How about the other matters?"

The talk went its way into the other matters. Rivers was quite out of his reverie, brusque, cynical, and sensible as usual. He snarled over the cigars in his invariable fashion with Randall and Jamieson. "You boys never *will* learn to pick out a decent cigar," he growled, flinging away half of Jamieson's latest sacrifice, "and I suppose if those Cuban niggers don't get put down, or can't put the Spaniards down, that there won't be any decent cigars left for anyone to smoke. It's sickening. Well, I'm going, now; and if I find that young monkey as close to the door as he was yesterday, I'm going to kick him!"

Randall and Jamieson looked at each other. "I suppose he has some money-making scheme in this," Randall ventured.

"I don't know," said Jamieson; "I know he's pulled us out of a hole."

Rivers found the office-boy near the door, but he did not kick him; he smiled sombrely at the brightness on the lad's face. "Got a mother and a lame sister, and looks like life and death to him, our keeping open, I expect," thought the old man. "No, there's too many of 'em; I couldn't do it. But—oh Lord! what'll Sissy say when she finds she ain't to have the house? Business losses it'll have to go to. Glad I didn't tell her more'n a hint; she can't have her hopes up much. And, Lord! what will I have to think about, now, when I'm alone, riding over the bridge, now I haven't got Jabez?" He shut his mouth more tightly, as he gave Swift a scowl with his nod. Swift's heart ran down like a clock; for a second seemed to stop ticking.

"Guess that means we are going to shut down," he muttered; "old man feels awful bad. Don't know why I hoped he'd stop it; but I guess I did, or I wouldn't be feeling so disappointed. Well, I suppose I ought to be thankful I can afford to take a little vacation, myself. But there's all the other boys!"

His wrinkled brow unconsciously imitated Rivers, when he strode to the furnace, almost running down the office-boy, such was his abstraction.

"What the h—— do you want, splay-feet?" he cried, in the natural irritation of the moment.

"Order from the old man," answered the lad, beaming on him, unabashed. He gave the order, adding, without the pause of a comma, " Say, the shops ain't going to shut down! "

"*What!*" Swift shouted.

"·Old man says so. Going to lend us his own money. He's got a lot in the bank. Don't give me away. I heard 'em talking. Guess the old man sees big money in it, somewhere." Swift, grinding his teeth, made a dive at the rolls with his tongs. " You're knowing a lot, Billy," said he, in a caustic tone; " you are a very smart boy, and you're mother's very proud of you, but if I was you I'd skip my opinions on the old man. Seeing he's running the shops at his own expense; and we've all got to thank him we're not out of a job. And I happen to know that he's given up plans he thought a deal on, to do it. That's all, Billy. On your way back, you might skip over to the twelve-inch and tell Forbes."

Billy must have obeyed, for the turn was no sooner finished than the heater appeared at Swift's ear.

"Ain't it good news!" he cried; "but I wish I knew what made the old man change his mind. It ain't like the Riverses. Giving up what they are set on is wuss than drawing teeth to all the breed. I expect he's got some deep scheme, and he'll jest mint money!"

Swift had no time for answer before he was gone; and his sudden retreat was explained when Swift saw the old man himself, standing by the rolls, where Jabez was wont to stand, eyeing the mill. His full, florid face had not grown paler, but it wore a shrunken, haggard look, peculiar to such faces when men suffer. Swift felt his throat contract with ugly pain. Never had he longed to speak, to say something, to let the old man know, as he longed then. He swallowed once or twice, a mist got into his eyes, he grinned foolishly. " We—

turned out fifty thousand yesterday, sir," said he.

A flicker kindled in the old man's dull eyes; they changed, and rested on the roller.

"The Edgewater is a dandy mill," said Swift; "ain't a better run one, anywhere."

"I guess so," said the old man. Half turning, he added, gruffly, over his shoulder: "And you're a damn good fellow, Swift; and you always were!"

Then he lumbered off slowly, past the silent engines, his head sagging a little, as if he were in thought.

Swift watched him. "Lord, I hope he's got somebody home ain't so damfool clumsy as me, and can comfort him a bit for things. Like's not he'll never be able to buy that house, now; and, next to Jabez, his heart was jest set on it. And he's lost 'em both. And folks think he's doing this to make money! Well, it's a lonesome world!"

www.ingramcontent.com/pod-product-compliance
Lightning Source LLC
Chambersburg PA
CBHW032137230426
43672CB00011B/2368